The Harper Book of Christian Poetry

The
Harper Book
of Christian Poetry

Selected and Introduced by

ANTHONY S. MERCATANTE , comp.

1817

HARPER & ROW, PUBLISHERS
New York • Evanston • San Francisco • London

Illustrations by Anthony S. Mercatante.

The following poems have been especially translated for this volume:
"Youthful Shepherd" by Clement of Alexandria and "Vesper Hymn" by an anonymous third-century writer; from the Greek, by Stephen Marks. "Song of the Creatures" by Francis of Assisi; from the Italian, by Anthony S. Mercatante. "Sonetto" by Ludovico Ariosto; from the Italian, by G.-Gabriel Gisondi. "On a Black Night," "Oh, Life-Giving Flame of Love," and "Sum of Perfection" by John of the Cross; from the Spanish, by Anthony S. Mercatante. "The Soul that Longs for God" by John of the Cross; from the Spanish, by John R. Matthews. "The Dream of Mary," anonymous; from the Russian, by Stephen Marks. Esther's speech from Act 4 of *Esther* by Jean Racine; from the French, by G.-Gabriel Gisondi. "When Sadness and Weariness . . ." by Novalis, and "Lord! Only in Your Peace Can I Find Rest . . ." by Clemens Brentano; from the German, by Ronald J. Suter.

THE HARPER BOOK OF CHRISTIAN POETRY. Copyright © 1972 by Anthony S. Mercatante. All rights reserved. Printed in the United States of America. For information address Harper & Row, Publishers, Inc., 10 East 53rd Street, New York, N.Y. 10022. Published simultaneously in Canada by Fitzhenry & Whiteside Limited, Toronto.

FIRST EDITION

STANDARD BOOK NUMBER: 06–065560–7

LIBRARY OF CONGRESS CATALOG CARD NUMBER: 72–78051

Designed by C. Linda Dingler

The editor and the publisher wish to thank the following for permission to reprint certain poems in this anthology:

Constable Publishers for "Good Friday: The Third Nocturn" by Peter Abelard, and "The Word of the Cross" by Saint Paulinus of Nola, from *Medieval Latin Lyrics* by Helen Wadell. Reprinted by permission.

Doubleday & Company for "A Poor Christian Looks at the Ghetto" by Czeslaw Milosz, translated by the author, from *Post-War Polish Poetry* edited and translated by Czeslaw Milosz (1965).

Farrar, Straus & Giroux, Inc., Noonday Press for "Spin Love" by Adam Mickiewicz, translated by Kimball Flaccus in *Adam Mickiewicz: Selected Poems* edited by Clark Mills, copyright, 1956.

Harcourt Brace Jovanovich, Inc. for "Journey of the Magi" by T. S. Eliot, from *Complete Poems 1909–1962* by T. S. Eliot, copyright © 1963, 1964, by T. S. Eliot and reprinted by permission of Harcourt Brace Jovanovich, Inc. and Faber and Faber; "when god lets my body be" by e. e. cummings, copyright © 1923, 1951 by e. e. cummings and reprinted from his volume *Poems 1923–1954* by permission of Harcourt Brace Jovanovich, Inc.; "The Holy Innocents" by Robert Lowell, from *Lord Weary's Castle*, copyright © 1944, 1946, by Robert Lowell and reprinted by permission of Harcourt Brace Jovanovich, Inc.

Johns Hopkins Press for selection from "The Christ of Válazquez" by Miguel de Unamuno, from *Ten Centuries of Spanish Poetry* edited by Eleanor L. Turnbull. Reprinted by permission of the Johns Hopkins Press.

The Macmillan Company for "The Second Coming" by William Butler Yeats. Reprinted with permission of the Macmillan Company from *Collected Poems* by William Butler Yeats. Copyright 1924 by the Macmillan Company, renewed 1952 by Bertha Georgie Yeats. Permission also of A. P. Watt & Son, Mr. M. B. Yeats, and The Macmillan Co. of Canada (from *The Collected Poems of W. B. Yeats*).

New Ameican Library for selection from *The Inferno* by Dante, as translated by John Ciardi, copyright © 1954 by John Ciardi; selection from *The Purgatorio* by Dante, as translated by John Ciardi, copyright © 1957, 1959, 1960, 1961 by John Ciardi; selection from *The Paradiso* by Dante, as translated by John Ciardi, copyright © 1961, 1967, 1970 by John Ciardi. Reprinted by arrangement with the New American Library, Inc., New York, New York.

New Directions Publishing Corp. for "And death shall have no dominion" by Dylan Thomas. Dylan Thomas, *Collected Poems*. Copyright 1943 by New Directions Publishing Corporation. Reprinted by permission of New Directions Publishing Corporation. Permission also of J. M. Dent & Sons Ltd. and the Trustees for the copyrights of the late Dylan Thomas (from *Collected Poems of Dylan Thomas*).

W. W. Norton & Company, Inc. for "Birth of Mary" and "Joseph's Suspicion" by Rainer Maria Rilke. Reprinted from *Translations from the Poetry of Rainer Maria Rilke* by M. D. Herter Norton, copyright 1938 by W. W. Norton & Company, Inc. Copyright 1966 by M. D. Herter Norton. Permission also of the Hogarth Press, London. Translation available in Canada is that by J. B. Leishmann, published by the Hogarth Press.

To Richard D. Brett

"Tu se' lo mio maestro. . . ."

Contents

Foreword

The present anthology offers a selection of the poetry produced by Christianity since its inception. The main emphasis has naturally fallen on those countries in Western Europe where Christianity has had its longest life and greatest cultural impact—Italy, Spain, Germany, France and England—though other centers of Christian culture such as Russia, Poland and Scandinavia, have been represented.

So that the reader may follow the development of Christian poetry from its earliest stages to the present, the book is arranged chronologically and is divided into eight sections: Early Christian, Medieval, Renaissance, Baroque, Neo-Classical, Romantic, Victorian, and Modern poetry. Each of the sections contains a selection of lyric and shorter poems and at least one extended work that mirrors the age in which it was written. Thus, in the Renaissance section, not only are sonnets of Petrarch and Michelangelo included but also the complete "An Hymn of Heavenly Love" of Spenser.

A Christian poet is in no better position than his non-Christian counterpart to write aesthetically satisfying poetry. Therefore, the main guiding principle in the collection has been to choose poems of high artistic worth. The personal beliefs of each poet, whether "orthodox" or not, have not entered into the selection. What has is whether or not their poetry explores some aspect of the Christian experience and whether or not it does so in aesthetically satisfying terms.

Regarding the poems themselves, I have held to the idea that a poem must be experienced as an entity. The use of truncated versions of longer poems has been avoided wherever possible. Since the anthology contains not only English and American poems but also translations from the Greek, Latin, Spanish, Italian, Russian, French, Gaelic, German, Polish,

Dutch, Swedish, Danish, and Portuguese in contemporary spelling and punctuation, modernized texts have been used for earlier English poems. In only a few instances, where it would violate the work to alter spelling or punctuation, have archaic spellings been retained.

Of course, the compiler of an anthology cannot hope to please everyone. It is my hope, however, that readers will find the selections stimulating and rewarding both as poetry and as expressions of Christian consciousness.

I would like to take this opportunity to express my thanks to the following: Marie Cantlon of Harper & Row, who believed in the work; Gary-Gabriel Gisondi for his valuable critical comments as well as translations; John R. Matthews for his translation of one poem of John of the Cross as well as his reading of the galleys; Toni Rachiele, who typed the manuscript; Miriam Vartanian for her aid with the manuscript; Professor Ronald Suter of Fairleigh Dickinson University for his translations; J.B. Singer for his valued assistance; Juan F. Montoya for the jacket photograph; and Susan Ann Protter for her help.

A.S.M.

Easter, 1972

Introduction

During the past two thousand years Christianity has inspired a vast body of art work—painting, music, architecture, and literature—which rivals that of any other culture, secular or religious. Among Christianity's most aesthetically satisfying creations is its poetry, claiming some of the greatest poets in Western literature, such as Dante and Milton.

These two poets, along with others, have drawn upon Christian culture in the creation of their poetry. Milton, for example, in his "Hymn on the Morning of Christ's Nativity," makes the birth of Jesus the nucleus for an elaborately rich and complex Baroque poem, which is filled with both Christian and secular symbolism, to explore the meaning of the Incarnation. Dante's *Divine Comedy* combines medieval Christian symbolism and secular learning to construct a monumental poem which delves into the mysteries of Faith and Knowledge.

These works of Milton and Dante represent but two ways in which poets have approached the writing of Christian verse. In contrast to them, John of the Cross, the Spanish mystic, in poems such as "Dark Night" and "Oh! Life-Giving Flame of Love," examines the nature of mystical union with God, using no overt Christian symbolism except that of Lover and Beloved, familiar to his readers from the Song of Songs in the Old Testament.

The force that unifies such divergent poetical personalities as Milton, Dante, and John of the Cross (as well as all Christian poets, irrespective of their artistic sensibilities and gifts) is their belief in the ultimate redemptive power of love as manifested in Jesus. It is this belief that makes their poetry "Christian" and finally brings them all to the foot of the Cross.

The early Church Fathers were too busy struggling with the world, the flesh, and the devil to encourage the writing of poetry. In fact, some early Fathers looked with suspicion upon poetry, regarding it as a pagan pastime that could only lead the faithful into sin. Augustine, in his *Confessions*, reprimanded himself because he was more moved by the plight of Dido in Virgil's *Aeneid* than by the sinful state of his own soul. His admonition against poetry as diverting the Christian from his true goal, namely, the salvation of his soul, was accepted by many theologians, though it did not deter the early Christians from writing poetry. Ambrose, his close friend and the bishop who received Augustine into the Church, composed numerous hymn-poems for church services, among which the beautiful *Aeterne rerum conditor* is still sung in the Daily Offices in many parts of the Western Church.

Previous to Ambrose's hymn-poems were works such as "Youthful Shepherd" ascribed to Clement of Alexandria and "Vesper Hymn" by an anonymous writer of the third century. Earlier still are the fragments of hymn-poems quoted by Paul in his letters (for example, Philippians 2:6–11 and Colossians 1:15–20). Paul even goes so far as to include a line from a pagan poet, Epimenides of Knossos (Titus 1:12) in one short epistle.

Luke the Evangelist, however, is recognized as the first Christian poet, an honor given him for the artistic excellence of the three poems included in his Gospel: the *Magnificat, Benedictus,* and *Nunc Dimittis.* (The titles come from the opening words in their Latin translation.) Luke's work relies heavily on the past. His poetry is saturated with both the language and imagery of the Old Testament (which he probably read in a Greek translation and not in the original Hebrew) as well as the current vernacular Greek spoken and written in most of the Mediterranean Roman empire. The *Magnificat,* for example, is filled with echoes of the Song of Hannah from the First Book of Samuel in the Old Testament. Luke's poem makes use of this earlier, traditional material but instills in it a tender, new, personal note that is characteristic of his entire Gospel. Building the *Magnificat* upon the revelation of God as he is manifested in the Old Testament poem, Luke reinterprets the poem in the light of God's revelation in the person of Jesus Christ. His poem thereby forms a bridge between the two Testaments.

Luke's method of using traditional materials has served many other Christian poets from earliest times to the present. Eliot's "Journey of the Magi," for instance, makes use of the technique in its opening lines:

> A cold coming we had of it,
> Just the worst time of the year
> For a journey, and such a long journey:
> The ways deep and the weather sharp,
> The very dead of winter,

which is a reworking of a passage from a Christmas sermon by Lancelot Andrewes, a seventeenth-century Anglican bishop, whose work Eliot admired. The sermon opens:

> A cold coming they had of it at this time of the year,
> just the worst time of the year to take a journey, and
> specially a long journey. The ways deep, the weather sharp,
> the days short, the sun farthest off, in *solstitio brumali*
> "the very dead of winter."

(Luke's and Eliot's poetics should make one reassess what it means to be "original," a term that has been inordinately praised since the Romantic movement in the nineteenth century.)

Many of the poets who followed Luke, such as Ambrose and Prudentius, to name but two, lack the subtlety of his thought as well as the richness of his vision. Part of this artistic deficiency is owing to the circumstances surrounding the creation of much early Christian poetry. The early hymn-poems were often occasional pieces; that is, poems written for specific church services, which expressed the corporate hope of the Christian community. These particular works, therefore, in their use of language and imagery tend to be less complex than the more individualistic poems of later Christian poets.

Light, Time, and the Last Judgment or Parousia (i.e., Second Coming of Christ)—the recurring themes and images used in these early poems —combine to express a linear concept of history which was at variance with the cyclical concept of pagan writers. Christian poetry from Ambrose past Eliot expresses this concept of history, whereas much secular poetry, though not all, still retains the pagan concept.

The early Christians existed in a world that was hostile to their basic beliefs. But once Christianity was established as the official religion of the Roman empire under Constantine in the fourth century, the

Church began to exert a powerful influence on society. While the Church continued to grow, however, the Western empire began to decline after Constantine had reestablished his capitol (at the newly created city of Byzantium) and came to an end in the fifth century when its emperor ceded all power to his Eastern counterpart. (The Eastern empire endured a thousand years after the fall of the West.)

The resulting social upheaval left its mark on Christian poetry, for little if any poetry of great artistic worth was to appear until the early Middle Ages, when numerous Anglo-Saxon Christian poems were written, among them the intensely moving poem "The Dream of the Cross."

Historians no longer label this nearly thousand-year period of European history as the Dark Ages; though the years following the collapse of the Western empire, when hordes of northern invaders ransacked most of the south, does lend itself to that description. But by the eighth century, with the reforms of Charlemagne, the culture of the Middle Ages began to form a coherent whole. The picture that emerges is a complex one, difficult for twentieth-century man to understand completely. While historians have amassed much factual information about the Middle Ages and we are in possession of much of its literature and art, we cannot possibly enter into the ethos of the period. Some writers and artists of the nineteenth century, under the influence of Romanticism, did make the attempt by initiating various "Gothic" revivals in the arts, seeking a return to the spirit of the earlier period. But, at best, what they produced were most often papier-mâché architecture, lifeless paintings, and mechanical flat verse. The Pre-Raphaelite brotherhood in England and the Nazarene school of painting in Germany perhaps best exemplify this failure.

But we have long given up this approach to the past as a means of valid artistic expression, realizing that the ethos of an age or culture consists of more than copying its tangible forms. The great difficulty in understanding the ethos of the Middle Ages stems from the separation of the "secular" from the "religious" which our culture inherits from the late Renaissance. With its advances in science and new awareness of pagan culture, the Renaissance brought this dichotomy to the fore; by the seventeenth century it had become part of Western man's emotional and social makeup.

Medieval man, however, for good or ill, did not suffer from this split personality of the secular and the religious. He could conceive of his God and saints as everyday people in the dress of his time; portray the Virgin and Child as mother and child, and not worry about whether his painting was historically "correct." As a believer, he was not interested in the "historical Jesus" but the Jesus of faith. Only with the nearly complete loss of faith experienced by many Christians in the nineteenth century did man feel the need to discover the "historical Jesus."

Faith helped supply medieval society with a firm base—one that lasted hundreds of years. The forces at work in the society strove for a unified vision of the universe, producing such works as Chartres Cathedral and Dante's *Divine Comedy*. Dante's poem, which achieved new life in the 1920s in the English-speaking world through T. S. Eliot's essays, attempts to capture the ethos of the Middle Ages. Based on a hierarchical order of theology and philosophy, the characters in the work are judged in conformity with set beliefs and systems, yet each character expresses a complex personality, without ever becoming a medieval textbook.

Although Dante's poem had great influence on subsequent European poetry, his philosophical and theological system did not bind all medieval artists. Chaucer, an equally great poet, in his massive work *The Canterbury Tales* shuns a hierarchical order and stays earthbound by avoiding strict moral judgments of his characters. Yet both Dante and Chaucer believe in the Incarnation, seek and are found by God—but each in his own manner. The Middle Ages was able to accommodate both systems, since at the base of each lies belief in the ultimate redemptive power of Love. Such love, whether for a woman as in Dante's poem, or for the diverse canvas of personalities in Chaucer's work, is merely a single aspect of the great love—the love of God for man, as manifested in Jesus Christ. It is, for example, the underlying belief in such poems as "A Dream of the Cross," by an anonymous eighth-century Anglo-Saxon poet, and the thirteenth-century Italian poem of Jacopo da Lentino, "Of His Lady in Heaven."

In emphasizing the redemptive power of love the Middle Ages rediscovered the role of woman in God's plan for man's salvation. While the early Church had condemned her as responsible for the fall of man, the Middle Ages could envision woman as an integral part of God's creation. The veneration of the Virgin Mary was, in part, the cause of this reevaluation of woman. Churches throughout Europe were dedicated to the Virgin, and numerous poems were written in her honor, such as Juan Ruiz's "Hymn to the Virgin." Her power over man's creative imagination (as virgin-mother-intercessor) did not end with the Middle Ages but extends to our own time. She is, for example, the central motif in Rainer Maria Rilke's "Mary" and "Joseph's Suspicion."

Dante's portrait of his beloved Beatrice in *La Vita Nuova* and the *Divine Comedy* gives greatest expression to the medieval concept. In each of these works Dante recalls the Beatrice he knew and loved. In the *Divine Comedy*, however, she is, apart from her "real" personality, also a representative of theology. Dante's fusion of the real and the symbolic in his portrait of Beatrice is one of the great achievements of his poetry.

The medieval striving for a unified concept of the universe, often called the Gothic Summation, could not, however, maintain its hold over society against the onslaught of scientific discoveries and the evolution of the modern secular state that began in the early part of the Renaissance.

The Renaissance has held a fascination for scholars and laymen since Burckhardt's *Civilization of the Renaissance in Italy*, Symonds's *Renaissance in Italy*, and Pater's *Studies in the History of the Renaissance* were published in the nineteenth century. Under the influence of these works, the art and architecture of the Renaissance became the yardstick by which Western man was to judge art works until the early part of the present century, when a reevaluation of aesthetics caused the Renaissance ideal to be questioned.

While historians still debate the supposed "beginning" of the Italian Renaissance, a general consensus points to the early fourteenth century, the period in which man's idea of his place in the universe underwent a significant change. The physical world was no longer merely a symbol of a spiritual world as it had been for some medieval thinkers, but a "reality" that could be confronted, mastered, and understood without the aid of divine intervention. The natural world was therefore "good" because it was within man's power to control it. The world state envisioned by Dante yielded to the Renaissance ideal of the national state ruled by a prince. As a result of this new emphasis on man's ability to control his destiny, the division between the secular and the religious became more pronounced in man's consciousness.

For a time, however, the new humanist attitude of the Renaissance produced a marriage of secular and religious thought. Nevertheless, this marriage was short-lived, for if we compare a sonnet of Petrarch with one by Michelangelo, we can see the complete breakup in sensibility. In Petrarch's sonnets the music is liquid, and his meaning reasonably clear. Michelangelo, on the other hand, presents a jagged sound, his thought is often concentrated and ambiguous. Clearly by Michelangelo's time the Renaissance union of secular and religious thought had collapsed. (It is interesting to note that when Wordsworth translated some of Michelangelo's sonnets he commented that one sonnet by the poet caused him more trouble than a whole book of Tasso's epic poem *Jerusalem Delivered.*)

The sonnet emerged during the Renaissance as the most important lyric form. From Italy it passed to England, France, and Spain, to become the mainstay of both religious and secular verse. Along with the development of the sonnet came a revived interest in narrative poetry, the Renaissance producing its share of Christian epics to rival that of the Middle Ages. Ariosto's *Orlando Furioso* and Tasso's *Jerusalem Delivered* (loved by Queen Elizabeth I and James I in Fairfax's translation) influenced nearly all subsequent Christian epic poetry from Spenser's *Faerie Queene* to Milton's *Paradise Lost.* Renaissance poets wished not only to edify but also to entertain their audiences, and their epic verse accordingly differs from its medieval counterparts by its richness of detail and outright romantic sensuousness.

Initially all new developments in the arts, science, and philosophy of the Renaissance were encouraged by the Church. In a short time, however, the Church realized the new learning meant that its organization would be open to question. Eventually more questions arose than the Church could cope with successfully. Corruption was everywhere and voices cried out for reform—drastic reform. For the most part the voices went unheeded. As a result a massive religious reformation split Europe into a Protestant north and a Catholic south.

While both sides plotted, warred, and countercharged each other the inner life of the Christian grew more intense. If we compare the poems of Francis Xavier, John Calvin, Teresa of Avila, Martin Luther, and John of the Cross, we see no denominational bias but an intensity of religious feeling that is common to all.

Because of continuing advances in science, the increasing power of the state, and the ever-widening gap between Protestant and Catholic thought, the seventeenth-century Christian found himself with no solid social or religious base. With the unity of the Middle Ages lost, and the hope of the early Renaissance shattered, the poetry of the seventeenth century became an intensely subjective medium of expression. Baroque poetry (to use the broader European term, as opposed to "metaphysical," which is usually applied to seventeenth-century English verse) represents the triumph of the poet's personality over a universal, or philosophical, system supported by either state or Church.

While, for instance, we know very little of Shakespeare's inner life from his sonnets or plays, we know a great deal of the life and beliefs of Donne from his poetry. The Baroque poet par excellence, Donne is intense, witty, personal, religious, erotic, and often obtuse—making of himself the chief protagonist in his verse. These qualities vary in degree with each Baroque poet, yet each possesses these qualities to some degree.

The complexity of Baroque verse eventually caused an artistic reaction in the next age—the Neo-Classical. For alongside Baroque mentality was another tradition, exemplified in English literature by Ben Jonson, which sought to avoid pitfalls inherent in the Baroque style. The differences between the two mentalities can be seen by comparing Donne's poem to God the Father with Jonson's poem on the same subject.

Although much critical writing has been devoted to exploring the harmony, control, and elegance of Neo-Classical verse, not enough attention has been paid to its often intense emotion, as evidenced in such a work as Pope's "Eloisa to Abelard." Too often we have been led to conceive of the Neo-Classicists as men immersed in Greek and Roman classics, losing sight of the fact that they were men of the world, often deeply committed to the Christian ideal, and sometimes at deep personal cost.

Pope maintained his Roman Catholic allegiance though it meant social hardship for him. Dryden converted to Catholicism, which cost him dearly in an English Protestant society. Swift, an Anglican priest and a friend of Pope, never could accommodate himself to English court life and so lived in exile in Ireland, where he eventually died insane. Across the English Channel Racine devoted his last two plays to biblical subjects—*Esther* and *Athalie*—while Corneille translated the *Imitation of Christ* into French.

Neo-Classical poets believed that Christianity and reason were compatible. Their belief was not shared by the generation that followed them. It is one of the tragedies of Western culture that the Romantic movement produced so little in the way of great Christian poetry, aside from one genius, William Blake.

Blake stands out as a Christian and a major poet of the Romantic movement, yet his contemporaries, Christian and non-Christian, thought him mad. He represents the Christian individualist, a troublesome creature to establishment Christianity and a man who always had a difficult time with his fellow Christians. Blake's personal vision of what it means to be a Christian in an unchristian world could never achieve popularity, either with his contemporaries or with those who followed him. His stress on the individual's commitment to God, as manifested in Jesus, demands too much from the Christian who wants his commitments verified in an external authority.

Most major Romantic poets—Keats, Shelley, Byron, Wordsworth, Poe, Goethe, Hugo—rejected nineteenth-century Christianity. Keats escaped into his dream world where truth and beauty were one, Wordsworth sought solace in nature, Shelley and Goethe in a revived Hellenism, Byron and Poe in an exploration of the senses, and Hugo in a philosophy that merged Eastern and Western thought.

The Victorians, who followed the Romantics, inherited from their predecessors a sense of loss that had overtaken Western society when the enthusiasm of the Age of Reason had collapsed in the wake of the French Revolution. Along with this philosophical burden, the Victorians also experienced the shock of rapid changes brought about by the growth of industrialism. An entirely new society was forming at such a fast pace that many of the old systems of thought no longer satisfied the questioning mind. Darwinian theory had such an impact on English and American minds, causing confusion and dismay to many who could not accommodate themselves to the new theories. The effect of so many changes was tremendous. The Victorian Christian had to rethink his role now as a Christian in a materialist society. Some Christian groups responded with a return to earlier forms of Christian expression. Various evangelical movements, for example, arose in Europe and America in response to the vacuum left by the established churches' inability to fulfill the spiritual needs of many Christians in the latter part of the eighteenth century.

In England, the High Church party, begun by the Oxford Movement, pumped new blood into a lifeless governmental church. The Oxford Movement began as a means of restoring to the English Church some of the vigor it had possessed in previous centuries. Through its publications, numerous translations from the works of the early Church became part of the Protestant tradition. John Keble and John Mason Neale, though no poets in their own right, helped disseminate numerous early Christian hymns through their translations from Greek and Latin. Many of their translations are still found in our hymnbooks today. The vigor of the Oxford Movement was matched by the continuing efforts of the evangelicals, who were mainly responsible for the emancipation of the slaves in the British empire. Today, the two traditions are closer than ever with the great emphasis on Christian unity.

The two most important poets of Victorian England, Browning and Tennyson, are also the major Christian poets produced in the latter part of the nineteenth century. (Hopkins, though of the same era, was not published until 1918 and belongs emotionally to our time.)

Browning's reputation is well established today, though there are still some critics who label his poetry "barbarous," as did Santayana. What were once considered his faults—poor diction, confused syntax, obscurity—appeal to many twentieth-century readers who can discern Browning's influence on much contemporary poetry. Browning grows out of the Elizabethans, Donne, and the English metaphysical poets, as opposed to Tennyson, who follows the stream from Spenser through Keats and the early Romantics.

Tennyson, in spite of his retiring nature and official position of poet laureate, struggled with the questions of belief that haunted his contemporaries after the Darwinian revolution. *In Memoriam*, his major work, is not what pious-minded nineteenth-century readers imagined—a balm to all their spiritual ills, a leatherbound volume to be laid on the mantelpiece for all to see. Tennyson's poem has been compared to Eliot's *The Waste Land* by some modern critics who point out the suffering and loss of faith that runs through the lyrics making up the sequence. We realize now that one has to be spiritually purged to enter finally into *In Memoriam*; then and only then can one call upon the "Strong Son of God" as does the poet.

Whereas Browning and Tennyson achieved popularity during their lifetimes, it took until the early part of the present century for the work of Gerard Manley Hopkins to gain recognition. This Jesuit priest, a convert to Roman Catholicism from Anglicanism (a road followed by many nineteenth-century Englishmen in the wake of the Oxford Movement) grappled with his God as Jacob with the Angel. The body of his work testifies to his quest to understand God's love as manifested in Jesus, amid a world that often seemed filled only with tragedy and contradiction.

Hopkins's poems were published in 1918; six years earlier Grierson's edition of Donne's poems had been made available to a new generation of English and American poets who had grown dissatisfied with Romanticism and Victorianism as valid artistic means of expression. Spurred on by the poetry of Hopkins and Donne, the new poets delved into Elizabethan and Jacobean literature as alternatives to the other traditions.

Their quest for new forms of expression coincided with a forced reevaluation of Western culture. Many poets viewed the First World War as the end of what they envisioned as Western civilization. These men now had to reassess all their basic beliefs and assumptions about the nature of Western society. Their pessimism was further aggravated by the rise of Fascism that swept Europe in the 1930s, culminating in another, even more costly war.

The poetry produced during the first half of the century reflects this emotional turmoil. Yet along with the pessimism of much twentieth-century poetry, came a new awareness of man's spiritual needs and longings. While our age has been called godless and wholly materialistic, it has nevertheless produced some of the most intense Christian poetry since the seventeenth century. Christianity has great meaning for such major modern poets as Eliot, Auden, Thomas, Rilke, Pasternak, cummings, Lowell, and Spender.

In 1869 Matthew Arnold wrote in *Culture and Anarchy:* "Hebraism and Hellenism,—between these two points of influence moves our world. At one time it feels more powerfully the attraction of one of them, at another time of the other." At the present we see the almost complete domination of our culture by the Hellenistic and, by extension, scientific stream, with its great emphasis on technological achievements.

Yet there are stirrings of dissatisfaction—the message of God's love as manifested in Jesus still haunts us, as it has haunted poets and thinkers for some two thousand years. Amid all the upheavals in our society Jesus still holds sway over us all and we cry with Paul: "*Maranatha*—O Lord, come!"

part one

Early Christian Poems

". . . The light shines, Christ is coming soon."

The fish, used early in Christian art, is a symbol of Christ. It derives its meaning, in part, from the Greek word for fish (*ichthus*), the initials of which form: Jesus Christ God's Son Savior. It is also used as a symbol of baptism, since the Christian needs the waters of baptism as a fish needs natural water in order to live, according to Tertullian.

Luke

(First century)

MAGNIFICAT

My soul doth magnify the Lord,
And my spirit hath rejoiced in God my Saviour.
For he hath regarded the lowliness of his handmaiden:
For behold, from henceforth all generations shall call me blessed.
For he that is mighty hath magnified me:
And holy is his name.
And his mercy is on them that fear him through-out all generations.
He hath showed strength with his arm,
He hath scattered the proud in the imagination of their hearts.
He hath put down the mighty from their seat:
And hath exalted the humble and meek.
He hath filled the hungry with good things:
And the rich he hath sent away empty.
He remembering his mercy, hath holpen his servant Israel:
As he promised to our forefathers, Abraham and his seed, for ever.

From the Greek, Book of Common Prayer, 1549

BENEDICTUS

Praise to the God of Israel!
For he has turned to his people, saved them and set them free,
And has raised up a deliverer of victorious power
from the house of his servant David.

3

So he promised: age after age he proclaimed
    by the lips of his holy prophets,
that he would deliver us from our enemies,
    out of the hands of all who hate us;
that he would deal mercifully with our fathers,
    calling to mind his solemn covenant.

Such was the oath he swore to our father Abraham,
    to rescue us from enemy hands,
and grant us, free from fear, to worship him
    with a holy worship, with uprightness of heart,
    in his presence, our whole life long.

And you, my child, you shall be called a Prophet of the Highest,
for you will be the Lord's forerunner, to prepare his way
    and lead his people to salvation through knowledge of him,
    by forgiveness of their sins:
for in the tender compassion of our God
    the morning sun from heaven will rise upon us,
to shine on those who live in darkness, under the cloud of death,
    and to guide our feet into the way of peace.

From the Greek, The New English Bible, 1970

NUNC DIMITTIS

Lord, now lettest thou thy servant depart
In peace, according to thy word:
For mine eyes have seen thy salvation,
Which thou hast prepared before the face of all people;
A light to lighten the Gentiles,
    And the glory of thy people Israel.

From the Greek, King James Version of the Bible, 1611

Attributed to Clement of Alexandria

(Ca.150–ca.215)

YOUTHFUL SHEPHERD

Youthful shepherd, guiding us by love and truth,
Christ-shepherd, our mighty King,
We come to sing your praises with sinless mouths—
"You are our holy Lord, the all-conquering Word,
The healer of all discord and master of our lives."

Youthful shepherd and helmsman, leader of the holy flock,
You are the great fisher of men, saving us by the bait of
Eternal life from the hostile waves of an evil sea!

Lead us, youthful shepherd, holy one, King of souls.
Lead us in your heavenly ways, O Word everlasting.
Lead us, master of time, eternal light, and fountain of mercy!

From the Greek, by Stephen Marks

Anonymous

(Third century)

VESPER HYMN

Hail, Jesus Christ,
bright and gracious light,
reflecting the glory of the everliving Father'

Now as the day fades into night,
and our eyes behold evening's light,
we sing your praises, great and loving God—
Father, Son and Holy Spirit!

To You, O Son of God, we give our praise,
for You are the giver of life,
the glory of all creation!

From the Greek, by Stephen Marks

Niceta of Remesiana

(335?–414)

TE DEUM LAUDAMUS

Thee, Sovereign God, our grateful accents praise;
We own thee Lord, and bless thy wondrous ways;
To thee, Eternal Father, earth's whole frame,
With loudest trumpets, sounds immortal fame.
Lord God of Hosts! for thee the heavenly powers
With sounding anthems fill the vaulted towers.
Thy Cherubims thrice, Holy, Holy, Holy, cry;
Thrice, Holy, all the Seraphims reply,
And thrice returning echoes endless songs supply.
Both heaven and earth thy majesty display;
They owe their beauty to thy glorious ray.
Thy praises fill the loud apostles' choir;
The train of prophets in the song conspire.
Legions of martyrs in the chorus shine,
And vocal blood with vocal music join.
By these thy church, inspir'd by heavenly art,
Around the world maintains a second part;
And tunes her sweetest notes, O God, to thee,
The Father of unbounded majesty;
The Son, ador'd copartner of thy seat,
And equal everlasting Paraclete.
Thou King of Glory, Christ, of the most high,
Thou coeternal filial Deity;
Thou who, to save the world's impending doom,
Vouchsaf'dst to dwell within a Virgin's womb;

Old tyrant Death disarm'd, before thee flew
The bolts of heaven, and back the foldings drew,
To give access, and make thy faithful way;
From God's right hand thy filial beams display.
Thou art to judge the living and the dead;
Then spare those souls for whom thy veins have bled.
O take us up amongst thy blest above,
To share with them thy everlasting love.
Preserve, O Lord, thy people, and enhance
Thy blessing on thine own inheritance.
For ever raise their hearts, and rule their ways;
Each day we bless thee, and proclaim thy praise:
No age shall fail to celebrate thy name,
No hour neglect thy everlasting fame.
Preserve our souls, O Lord, this day from ill;
Have mercy on us, Lord, have mercy still:
As we have hop'd, do thou reward our pain;
We've hop'd in thee—let not our hope be vain.

From the Latin, by John Dryden

Ambrose of Milan

(340?–397)

AETERNE RERUM CONDITOR

Framer of the earth and sky,
  Ruler of the day and night,
With a glad variety
  Tempering all, and making light;

Gleams upon our dark path flinging,
  Cutting short each night begun.
Hark! for chanticleer is singing,
  Hark! he chides the lingering sun.

And the morning star replies
  And lets loose the imprisoned day;

7

And the godless bandit flies
  From his haunt and from his prey.

Shrill it sounds; the storm relenting
  Soothes the weary seaman's ears;
Once it wrought a great repenting
  In that flood of Peter's tears.

Rouse we; let the blithesome cry
  Of that bird our hearts awaken,
Chide the slumbers as they lie,
  And arrest the sin o'ertaken.

Hope and health are in his strain
  To the fearful and the ailing;
Murder sheathes his blade profane;
  Faith revives when faith was failing.

Jesu, Master! when we sin
  Turn on us Thy healing face;
It will melt the offence within
  Into penitential grace.

Beam on our bewildered mind
  Till its dreamy shadows flee:
Stones cry out where Thou has shined,
  Jesu! musical with Thee.

To the Father and the Son
  And the Spirit, who in heaven
Ever witness, Three in One,
  Praise on earth be ever given.

From the Latin, by John Henry Newman

Aurelius Prudentius Clemens

(348–410?)

THE SECOND HYMN: A MORNING HYMN

Night and dark and the clouds of night,
the world's confusion and trouble:
be gone. The morning star appears,
the light shines, Christ is coming soon.

The murkiness of earth is pierced
by a stroke of the sun's spear; now
the colours return to all things
as the face of the sun rises.

The darkness in us will be torn.
The heart that has felt its own sin
will be cleared as the clouds break up
and be brightened in God's kingdom.

Then we will not be permitted
to hide the swarthy thoughts we think
but in the newness of morning
the heart's secrets will be opened.

In that time just before dawn
thieves have no fear of punishment
while light, enemy of deceit,
reveals theft in its hiding place.

Sly and expert deception loves
to be shrouded in darkness while
the lover prizes night's blackness
because it is right for his deed.

Behold, the flaming sun rises
to shame, to sadden and to judge

9

because there is no man who sins
easily under the sun's eye.

Can anyone refuse to blush
when he thinks of what he has drunk?
Desire is weak in the morning
when even the wicked are pure.

Now is the time to be austere.
Let no one take up foolishness.
Now all men put a serious
face on the follies they attempt.

This is the time when it is best
that all men be industrious,
whether soldier or citizen,
sailor, workman, ploughman or clerk.

One seeks fame in the courts of law,
another hears the bugle's call.
Both the merchant and the farmer
sigh greedily for their profits.

But we, ignorant of income
or interest or persuasive speech
or even the bravery of war,
are proud that we know only Christ.

We have learned to approach you on
bent knee with pure and simple minds
weeping and singing all the while
in our devout voices and songs.

This is the trade that makes us rich;
these are the deals by which we live.
These are the riches we begin
to work for when the sun appears.

Carefully inspect our feelings;
see every moment of our lives.
Many foul stains can be found there
much in need of your cleansing light.

Allow us to persevere and
let your light shine as you told us
when we were washed in the Jordan
and our uncleanness flowed away.

Whatever the night of the world
has darkened since then with its clouds,
we pray you, O King, brighten it
with the radiance of your face,

O Holy One. Just as tar turns
to milk and ebony turns to
crystal before your eyes, so can
you wipe away all stain of sin.

It was beneath the gloom of night
that Jacob wrestled so boldly
with an angel stronger than he
until the sun rose in the sky.

When the morning light touched his skin,
his knee buckled and he was lamed.
Defeated by that weakness, he
was no longer able to sin.

His thighs were deprived of that strength
which lurks in the lower body,
in the place where lust is enshrined,
far away from the heart's control.

These stories tell us that all men
buried in darkness lose their strength
to keep up the struggle with sin
unless they give in to God's strength.

That man whom the daylight revealed
crippled and severely weakened
after his nocturnal struggle
is the man who is more blessed.

May the blindness which has allowed
us to fall in danger and led

our feet away from the footpath
be gone; may our vision be clear;

    may this morning light illumine
our day and purify our souls.
Let our tongues form no devious words;
let our minds harbour no dark thoughts.

    May all of this day pass so that
neither our tongues nor our hands nor
our shifty eyes may commit sin.
May our bodies be free of guilt.

    There is one who sees from above
and stands there watching everything
that we do and are through the day.
His lonely vigil has no end.

    He is both our witness and judge.
All things that a man's mind conceives
he is careful to consider
because he is never deceived.

From the Latin, by Harold Isbell

Paulinus of Nola

(353–431)

THE WORD OF THE CROSS

Look on thy God, Christ hidden in our flesh.
A bitter word, the cross, and bitter sight:
Hard rind without, to hold the heart of heaven.
Yet sweet it is; for God upon that tree
Did offer up his life: upon that rood
My Life hung, that my life might stand in God.
Christ, what am I to give Thee for my life?
Unless take from Thy hands the cup they hold,
To cleanse me with the precious draught of death.

What shall I do? My body to be burned?
Make myself vile? The debt's not paid out yet.
Whate'er I do, it is but I and Thou,
And still do I come short, still must Thou pay
My debts, O Christ; for debts Thyself hadst none.
What love may balance Thine? My Lord was found
In fashion like a slave, that so His slave
Might find himself in fashion like his Lord.
Think you the bargain's hard, to have exchanged
The transient for the eternal, to have sold
Earth to buy Heaven? More dearly God bought me.

From the Latin, by Helen Waddell

Patrick of Ireland

(377–460)

LORICA, or THE BREASTPLATE

I arise today
Through a mighty strength, the invocation of the Trinity,
Through a belief in the Threeness,
Through confession of the Oneness
Of the Creator of creation.
I arise today
Through the strength of Christ's birth and His baptism,
Through the strength of His crucifixion and His burial,
Through the strength of His resurrection and His ascension,
Through the strength of His descent for the judgment of doom.
I arise today
Through the strength of the love of cherubim,
In obedience of angels,
In service of archangels,
In the hope of resurrection to meet with reward,
In prayers of patriarchs,
In predictions of prophets,
In preachings of apostles,

In faiths of confessors,
In innocence of virgins,
In deeds of righteous men.
I arise today
Through the strength of heaven;
Light of the sun,
Radiance of the moon,
Splendor of fire,
Speed of lightning,
Swiftness of the wind,
Depth of the sea,
Stability of the earth,
Firmness of the rock.
I arise today
Through God's strength to pilot me;
God's might to uphold me,
God's wisdom to guide me,
God's eye to look before me,
God's ear to hear me,
God's word to speak for me,
God's hand to guard me,
God's way to lie before me,
God's shield to protect me,
God's hosts to save me
From snares of the devil,
From temptations of vices,
From every one who desires me ill,
Afar or anear,
Alone or in a multitude.
I summon today all these powers between me and evil,
Against every cruel merciless power that opposes my body and soul,
Against incantations of false prophets,
Against black laws of pagandom,
Against false laws of heretics,
Against craft of idolatry,
Against spells of women and smiths and wizards,
Against every knowledge that corrupts man's body and soul.
Christ shield me today

Against poison, against burning,
Against drowning, against wounding,
So that reward may come to me in abundance.
Christ with me, Christ before me, Christ behind me,
Christ in me, Christ beneath me, Christ above me,
Christ on my right, Christ on my left,
Christ when I lie down, Christ when I sit down,
Christ when I arise,
Christ in the heart of every man who thinks of me,
Christ in the mouth of every man who speaks of me,
Christ in the eye that sees me,
Christ in the ear that hears me.
I arise today
Through a mighty strength, the invocation of the Trinity,
Through a belief in the Threeness,
Through a confession of the Oneness
Of the Creator of creation.

Anonymous translation from the Gaelic

Anicius Boethius

(Ca.480–ca.524)

O QUI PERPETUA MUNDUM RATIONE GUBERNAS

O thou, whose all-creating hands sustain
The radiant Heav'ns, and Earth, and ambient main!
Eternal Reason! whose presiding soul
Informs great nature and directs the whole!
Who wert, e're time his rapid race begun,
And bad'st the years in long procession run:
Who fix't thy self amidst the rowling frame,
Gav'st all things to be chang'd, yet ever art the same!
Oh teach the mind t' aetherial heights to rise,
And view familiar, in its native skies,
The source of good; thy splendor to descry,
And on thy self, undazled, fix her eye.

15

Oh quicken this dull mass of mortal clay;
Shine through the soul, and drive its clouds away!
For thou art Light. In thee the righteous find
Calm rest, and soft serenity of mind;
Thee they regard alone; to thee they tend;
At once our great original and end,
At once our means, our end, our guide, our way,
Our utmost bound, and our eternal stay!

From the Latin, by Alexander Pope

Venantius Fortunatus

(Ca. 535–ca. 600)

THE CRUCIFIXION, or PANGE LINGUA

Frame, my tongue, a song of wonder,
    Let the noble numbers ring;
Sing the glorious triumph crowning
    Our Redeemer, Christ the King;
Sing the sacred immolation
    That from death revoked the sting.

By the tree the crime of Adam
    Plunged the earth in blighting sin;
From the tree man's woe was measured,
    All the evil lay therein;
On the tree, by God's appointment,
    Christ must die the world to win.

Thus the work of our salvation
    Was by law divine ordained,
Thus by good to ill opposing
    Was the tempter's power restrained;
Whence the evil, thence the healing,
    Whence came death true life is gained.

In his holy hour the Saviour
    From the halls of heaven is come,

Takes the flesh of human nature;
　　So to save the flesh from doom;
Born as man, the world's Creator
　　Issues from a virgin's womb.

In a stable poor and lowly,
　　He, a tender child is born,
With a manger for a cradle,
　　Our Redeemer lies forlorn;
Swathing him in bands, the mother
　　Shields the Babe from shame and scorn.

Thirty years are soon completed,
　　And the day of woe is nigh;
Comes the hour of man's redemption,
　　When the Christ is doomed to die;
On the cross, a lamb, uplifted,
　　Lo! the Lord of earth and sky!

With a crown of thorns they crown him,
　　And they nail him to the wood,
With a lance they pierce his body
　　Whence the water and the blood
Flow, till ocean, earth and heaven
　　Bathe in the redeeming flood.

Faithful cross, a tree so noble
　　Never grew in grove or wood;
Never leaf or blossom flourished
　　Fair as on thy branches glowed;
Sweet the wood and sweet the iron
　　Bearing up so dear a load.

Ah! relax thy native rigour,
　　Bend thy branches, lofty tree!
Melt, O wood, in tender mercy!
　　Christ, the King of Glory, see!
Veiled in human sin and sorrow,
　　Slain, from sin the world to free.

Thou alone art found all worthy
    Earth's dread sacrifice to bear;
Thus to save the world from ruin,
    And the way to heaven prepare;
By his sacred blood anointed
    Thou, O Tree, art wondrous fair.

Everlasting praise and glory
    To the blessed Trinity;
Glory to the heavenly Father,
    To the Son like glory be;
Glory to the Holy Spirit,
    God eternal, one in three.

From the Latin, by Daniel J. Donahoe

part two

Medieval Christian Poems

". . . The Love that moves the Sun and other stars."

The unicorn, a mythical beast, is sometimes used as a symbol of the Incarnation. Legend says that only a virgin could bring about the capture of the beautiful animal.

Caedmon

(Fl. 670)

A HYMN

Now we must praise the ruler of heaven,
The might of the Lord and His purpose of mind,
The work of the Glorious Father; for He
God Eternal, established each wonder,
He, Holy Creator, first fashioned the heavens
As a roof for the children of earth.
And then our Guardian, the everlasting Lord,
Adorned this middle-earth for men.
Praise the almighty King of Heaven.

Anonymous translation from the Anglo-Saxon

John of Damascus

(Ca.675–ca.749)

HYMN TO CHRIST

O Christ, a light transcendent
Shines in thy countenance,
And none can tell the sweetness,
The beauty of thy grace.

In this may thy poor servants
Their joy eternal find;

Thou calledst them, O rest them,
Thou Lover of mankind.

Anonymous translation from the Greek

Anonymous

(Eighth century)

A DREAM OF THE CROSS

Lo! I will tell the dearest of dreams
That I dreamed in the midnight when mortal men
Were sunk in slumber. Me-seemed I saw
A wondrous Tree towering in air,
Most shining of crosses compassed with light.
Brightly that beacon was gilded with gold;
Jewels adorned it fair at the foot,
Five on the shoulder-beam, blazing in splendour.
Through all creation the angels of God
Beheld it shining— no cross of shame!
Holy spirits gazed on its gleaming,
Men upon earth and all this great creation.
 Wondrous that Tree, that Token of triumph,
And I a transgressor soiled with my sins!
I gazed on the Rood arrayed in glory,
Shining in beauty and gilded with gold,
The Cross of the Saviour beset with gems.
But through the gold-work outgleamed a token
Of the ancient evil of sinful men
Where the Rood on its right side once sweat blood.
Saddened and rueful, smitten with terror
At the wondrous Vision, I saw the Cross
Swiftly varying vesture and hue,
New wet and stained with the Blood outwelling,
Now fairly jewelled with gold and gems.
 Then, as I lay there, long I gazed
In rue and sadness on my Saviour's Tree,

Till I heard in dream   how the Cross addressed me,
Of all woods worthiest,   speaking these words:
     "Long years ago   (well yet I remember)
They hewed me down   on the edge of the holt,
Severed my trunk;   strong foemen took me,
For a spectacle wrought me,   a gallows for rogues.
High on their shoulders   they bore me to hilltop,
Fastened me firmly,   an army of foes!
     "Then I saw the King   of all mankind
In brave mood hasting   to mount upon me.
Refuse I dared not,   nor bow nor break,
Though I felt earth's confines   shudder in fear;
All foes I might fell,   yet still I stood fast.
     "Then the young Warrior,   God, the All-Wielder,
Put off His raiment,   steadfast and strong;
With lordly mood   in the sight of many
He mounted the Cross   to redeem mankind.
When the Hero clasped me   I trembled in terror,
But I dared not bow me   nor bend to earth;
I must needs stand fast.   Upraised as the Rood
I held the High King,   the Lord of heaven.
I dared not bow!   With black nails driven
Those sinners pierced me;   the prints are clear,
The open wounds.   I dared injure none.
They mocked us both.   I was wet with blood
From the Hero's side   when He sent forth His spirit.
     "Many a bale   I bore on that hill-side
Seeing the Lord   in agony outstretched.
Black darkness covered   with clouds God's body,
That radiant splendour.   Shadow went forth
Wan under heaven;   all creation wept
Bewailing the King's death.   Christ was on the Cross.
     "Then many came quickly,   faring from far,
Hurrying to the Prince.   I beheld it all.
Sorely smitten with sorrow   in meekness I bowed
To the hands of men.   From His heavy and bitter pain
They lifted Almighty God.   Those warriors left me
Standing bespattered with blood;   I was wounded with spears.

23

Limb-weary they laid Him down;   they stood at His head,
Looked on the Lord of heaven   as He lay there at rest
From His bitter ordeal all forspent.   In sight of His slayers
They made Him a sepulchre   carved from the shining stone;
Therein laid the Lord of triumph.   At evening tide
Sadly they sang their dirges   and wearily turned away
From their lordly Prince;   there He lay all still and alone.
    "There at our station   a long time we stood
Sorrowfully weeping   after the wailing of men
Had died away.   The corpse grew cold,
The fair life-dwelling.   Down to earth
Men hacked and felled us,   a grievous fate!
They dug a pit   and buried us deep.
But there God's friends   and followers found me
And graced me with treasure   of silver and gold.
    "Now may you learn,   O man beloved,
The bitter sorrows   that I have borne,
The work of caitiffs.   But the time is come
That men upon earth   and through all creation
Show me honour   and bow to this sign.
On me a while   God's Son once suffered;
Now I tower under heaven   in glory attired
With healing for all   that hold me in awe.
Of old I was once   the most woeful of tortures,
Most hateful to all men,   till I opened for them
The true Way of life.   Lo! the Lord of glory,
The Warden of heaven,   above all wood
Has glorified me   as Almighty God
Has honoured His Mother,   even Mary herself,
Over all womankind   in the eyes of men.
    "Now I give you bidding,   O man beloved,
Reveal this Vision   to the sons of men,
And clearly tell   of the Tree of glory
Whereon God suffered   for man's many sins
And the evil that Adam   once wrought of old.
    "Death He suffered,   but our Saviour rose
By virtue of His great might   as a help to men.
He ascended to heaven.   But hither again

He shall come unto earth   to seek mankind,
The Lord Himself   on the Day of Doom,
Almighty God   with His angel hosts.
And then will He judge,   Who has power of judgment,
To each man according   as here on earth
In this fleeting life   he shall win reward.
   "Nor there may any   be free from fear
Hearing the words   which the Wielder shall utter.
He shall ask before many: Where is the man
Who would taste bitter death   as He did on the Tree?
And all shall be fearful   and few shall know
What to say unto Christ.   But none at His Coming
Shall need to fear   if he bears in his breast
This best of symbols;   and every soul
From the ways of earth   through the Cross shall come
To heavenly glory, who would dwell with God."
   Then with ardent spirit   and earnest zeal,
Companionless, lonely,   I prayed to the Cross.
My soul was fain of death.   I had endured
Many an hour of longing.   It is my life's hope
that I may turn   to this Token of triumph,
I above all men,   and revere it well.
   This is my heart's desire,   and all my hope
Waits on the Cross.   In this world now
I have few powerful friends;   they have fared hence
Away from these earthly gauds   seeking the King of glory,
Dwelling now with the High Father   in heaven above,
Abiding in rapture.   Each day I dream
Of the hour when the Cross of my Lord,   whereof here on earth
I once had vision,   from this fleeting life may fetch me
And bring me where is great gladness   and heavenly bliss,
Where the people of God   are planted and stablished for ever
In joy everlasting.   There may it lodge me
Where I may abide in glory   knowing bliss with the saints.
   May the Lord befriend me   who on earth of old
Once suffered on the Cross   for the sins of men.
He redeemed us, endowed us with life   and a heavenly home.
Therein was hope renewed   with blessing and bliss

For those who endured the burning.   In that great deed
God's Son was triumphant,   possessing power and strength!
Almighty, Sole-Ruling   He came to the kingdom of God
Bringing a host of souls   to angelic bliss,
To join the saints   who abode in the splendour of glory,
When the Lord, Almighty God,   came again to His throne.

From the Old English, by Charles W. Kennedy

Attributed to Rabanus Maurus

(784?–856)

VENI CREATOR SPIRITUS

Creator Spirit, by whose aid
The world's foundations first were laid,
Come visit ev'ry pious mind;
Come pour thy joys on humankind;
From sin and sorrow set us free,
And make thy temples worthy thee.
    O source of uncreated light,
The Father's promis'd Paraclete!
Thrice holy fount, thrice holy fire,
Our hearts with heav'nly love inspire;
Come, and thy sacred unction bring
To sanctify us, while we sing!
    Plenteous of grace, descend from high,
Rich in thy sev'nfold energy,
Thou strength of his almighty hand,
Whose pow'r does heav'n and earth command.
Proceeding Spirit, our defense,
Who dost the gifts of tongues dispense,
And crown'st thy gift with eloquence!
    Refine and purge our earthly parts;
But, O, inflame and fire our hearts!
Our frailties help, our vice control,
Submit the senses to the soul;
And when rebellious they are grown,

Then lay thy hand, and hold 'em down.
    Chase from our minds th' infernal foe,
And peace, the fruit of love, bestow;
And lest our feet should step astray,
Protect and guide us in the way.
    Make us eternal truths receive,
And practice all that we believe:
Give us thyself, that we may see
The Father and the Son, by thee.
    Immortal honor, endless fame,
Attend th' Almighty Father's name:
The Savior Son be glorified,
Who for lost man's redemption died;
And equal adoration be,
Eternal Paraclete, to thee.

From the Latin, by John Dryden

Anonymous

(Ninth century)

CHRIST, THERE IS A SWARM OF BEES . . .

Christ, there is a swarm of bees outside.
Fly hither, my little cattle,
In blest peace, in God's protection,
Come home safe and sound!
Sit down, sit down, Bee,
Saint Mary commanded thee.
Thou shalt not have leave,
Thou shalt not fly to the wood!
Thou shalt not escape me,
Nor go away from me.
Sit very still,
And wait God's will!

Anonymous translation from Old High German

Anonymous

(Eleventh century)

From LA CHANSON DE ROLAND

The Archbishop, who God loved in high degree,
Beheld his wounds all bleeding fresh and free;
And then his cheek more ghastly grew and wan,
And a faint shudder through his members ran.
Upon the battle-field his knee was bent!
Brave Roland saw, and to his succor went,
Straightway his helmet from his brow unlaced,
And tore the shining hauberk from his breast.
Then raising in his arms the man of God,
Gently he laid him on the verdant sod.
"Rest, Sire," he cried,—"for rest thy suffering needs."
The priest replied, "Think but of warlike deeds!
The field is ours; well may we boast this strife!
But death steals on,—there is no hope of life;
In paradise, where Almoners live again,
There are our couches spread, there shall we rest from pain."

Sore Roland grieved; nor marvel I, alas!
That thrice he swooned upon the thick green grass.
When he revived, with a loud voice cried he,
"O Heavenly Father! Holy Saint Marie!
Why lingers death to lay me in my grave!
Beloved France! how have the good and brave
Been torn from thee, and left thee weak and poor!"
Then thoughts of Aude, his lady-love, came o'er
His spirit, and he whispered soft and slow,
"My gentle friend!—what parting full of woe!
Never so true a liegeman shalt thou see;—
Whate'er my fate, Christ's benison on thee!
Christ, who did save from realms of woe beneath,

The Hebrew Prophets from the second death."
Then to the Paladins whom well he knew,
He went, and one by one unaided drew
To Turpin's side, well skilled in ghostly lore;—
No heart had he to smile, but, weeping sore,
He blessed them in God's name, with faith that he
Would soon vouchsafe to them a glad eternity.

The Archbishop, then, on whom God's benison rest,
Exhausted, bowed his head upon his breast;—
His mouth was full of dust and clotted gore,
And many a wound his swollen visage bore.
Slow beats his heart, his panting bosom heaves,
Death comes apace,—no hope of cure relieves.
Towards heaven he raised his dying hands and prayed
That God, who for our sins was mortal made,
Born of the Virgin, scorned and crucified,
In paradise would place him by his side.

Then Turpin died in service of Charlon,
In battle great and eke great orison;—
'Gainst Pagan host alway strong champion;
God grant to him his holy benison.

From the French, by Henry W. Longfellow

Peter Abelard

(1079–1142)

GOOD FRIDAY: THE THIRD NOCTURN

Alone to sacrifice Thou goest, Lord,
    Giving Thyself to death whom Thou wilt slay.
For us Thy wretched folk is any word,
    Whose sins have brought Thee to this agony?

For they are ours, O Lord, our deeds, our deeds,
    Why must Thou suffer torture for our sin?

29

Let our hearts suffer for Thy passion, Lord,
  That very suffering may Thy mercy win.

This is that night of tears, the three days' space,
  Sorrow abiding of the eventide,
Until the day break with the risen Christ,
  And hearts that sorrowed shall be satisfied.

So may our hearts share in Thine anguish, Lord,
  That they may sharers of Thy glory be:
Heavy with weeping may the three days pass,
  To win the laughter of Thine Easter Day.

From the Latin, by Helen Waddell

Attributed to Bernard of Clairvaux

(1090–1153)

JESU DULCIS MEMORIA

Jesus to cast one thought upon
Makes gladness after He is gone;
But more than honey and honeycomb
Is to come near and take Him home.

Song never was so sweet in ear,
Word never was such news to hear,
Thought half so sweet there is not one
As Jesus God the Father's Son.

Jesu, their hope who go astray,
So kind to those who ask the way,
So good to those who look for Thee,
To those who find what must Thou be?

To speak of that no tongue will do
Nor letters suit to spell it true
But they can guess who have tasted of
What Jesus is and what is love.

30

Jesu, a springing well Thou art,
Daylight to head and treat to heart,
And matched with Thee there's nothing glad
That men have wished for or have had.

Wish us good morning when we wake
And light us, Lord, with Thy daybreak.
Beat from our brains the thicky night
And fill the world up with delight.

Be our delight, O Jesu, now
As by and by our prize art Thou,
And grant our glorying may be
World without end alone in Thee.

From the Latin, by Gerard Manley Hopkins

Francis of Assisi

(Ca.1180–1226)

SONG OF THE CREATURES

Most high, almighty, good Lord,
    to you belongs praise, glory, honor, all blessings—
    to you alone, most high, belongs all reverence.
    No man can fully speak of all your wonders.

Be praised, my Lord, with all your creation—
    especially our brother the sun,
    who brings us day and light:
    He is beautiful and radiant with splendor.
    Most high, he is a symbol of you!

Be praised, my Lord, for our sister the moon and the stars:
    You have placed them in the heavens—clear, priceless, and
            beautiful.
Be praised, my Lord, for our brother the wind and for air,
    good weather, and seasons through which your whole
    creation lives.

Be praised, my Lord for our sister water,
    so useful, humble, precious, and chaste.
Be praised, my Lord for our brother fire,
    who brightens the darkness of night.
    He is beautiful, happy, robust and strong.
Be praised, my Lord, for our sister mother earth:
    she supports, nourishes, and gives forth vegetations—
    colorful flowers and grass.
Be praised, my Lord, for all those who forgive and understand
    one another for love of you—
    Those who bear sickness and suffering.
Happy are those who live at peace with one another.
They shall receive a crown from the Most High.

Be praised, my Lord for our sister bodily Death,
    from whom no man can escape.
        How sad those who die without you!
        Happy are those who follow your holy will—
            the second death shall be powerless to harm them.

Praise, blessings, thanksgiving to my Lord—
Let us serve Him with great love.

From the Italian, by Anthony S. Mercatante

Jacopo da Lentino

(Ca.1180–ca.1240)

OF HIS LADY IN HEAVEN

I have it in my heart to serve God so
    That into Paradise I shall repair,—
    The holy place through the which everywhere
I have heard say that joy and solace flow.
Without my lady I were loath to go,—
    She who has the bright face and the bright hair;
    Because if she were absent, I being there,
My pleasure would be less than nought, I know.

Look you, I say not this to such intent
    As that I there would deal in any sin:
    I only would behold her gracious mien,
    And beautiful soft eyes, and lovely face,
That so it should be my complete content
    To see my lady joyful in her place.

From the Italian, by Dante G. Rossetti

Attributed to Thomas of Celano

(Ca.1190–1260)

DIES IRAE

Hear'st thou, my soul, what serious things
Both the Psalm and Sibyl sings
Of a sure Judge, from whose sharp ray
The world in flames shall fly away!

O that Fire! before whose face
Heaven and earth shall find no place:
O those Eyes! whose angry light
Must be the day of that dread night.

O that Trump! whose blast shall run
An even round with th' circling Sun,
And urge the murmuring graves to bring
Pale mankind forth to meet his King.

Horror of Nature, Hell, and Death!
When a deep groan from beneath
Shall cry, "We come, we come!" and all
The caves of night answer one call.

O that book! whose leaves so bright
Will set the world in severe light.
O that Judge! whose hand, whose eye
None can endure, yet none can fly.

Ah then, poor soul! what wilt thou say?
And to what patron choose to pray,
When stars themselves shall stagger, and
The most firm foot no more then stand?

But Thou giv'st leave, dread Lord, that we
Take shelter from Thyself in Thee;
And with the wings of Thine own dove
Fly to Thy scepter of soft love!

Dear Lord, remember in that day
Who was the cause Thou cam'st this way;
Thy sheep was strayed, and Thou would'st be
Even lost Thyself in seeking me!

Shall all that labor, all that cost
Of love, and even that loss, be lost?
And this loved soul judged worth no less
Than all that way and weariness?

Just mercy, then, Thy reck'ning be
With my price, and not with me;
'Twas paid at first with too much pain
To be paid twice, or once in vain.

Mercy, my Judge, mercy I cry,
With blushing cheek and bleeding eye;
The conscious colors of my sin
Are red without, and pale within.

O let Thine own soft bowels pay
Thyself, and so discharge that day!
If Sin can sigh, Love can forgive,
O, say the word, my soul shall live!

Those mercies which Thy Mary found,
Or who Thy cross confess'd and crowned,
Hope tells my heart the same loves be
Still alive, and still for me.

Though both my prayers and tears combine,
Both worthless are, for they are mine;
But Thou Thy bounteous self still be,
And show Thou art by saving me.

O when Thy last frown shall proclaim
The flocks of goats to folds of flame,
And all Thy lost sheep found shall be,
Let "Come ye blessed" then call me!

When the dread "ITE" shall divide
Those limbs of death from Thy left side,
Let those life-speaking lips command
That I inherit Thy right hand!

O, hear a suppliant heart all crush'd
And crumbled into contrite dust!
My hope, my fear—my Judge, my Friend!
Take charge of me, and of my end!

From the Latin, by Richard Crashaw

Thomas Aquinas

(Ca. 1225–1274)

ADORO TE SUPPLEX, LATENS DEITAS

Godhead here in hiding, whom I do adore
Masked by these bare shadows, shape and nothing more,
See, Lord, at thy service low lies here a heart
Lost, all lost in wonder at the God thou art.

Seeing, touching, tasting are in thee deceived;
How says trusty hearing? that shall be believed:
What God's Son has told me, take for truth I do;
Truth himself speaks truly or there's nothing true.

On the cross thy godhead made no sign to men;
Here thy very manhood steals from human ken:

Both are my confession, both are my belief,
And I pray the prayer of the dying thief.

I am not like Thomas, wounds I cannot see,
But can plainly call thee Lord and God as he:
This faith each day deeper be my holding of,
Daily make me harder hope and dearer love.

O thou our reminder of Christ crucified,
Living Bread of life of us for whom he died,
Lend this life to me then: feed and feast my mind,
There be thou the sweetness man was meant to find.

Bring the tender tale true of the Pelican;
Bathe me, Jesu Lord, in what thy bosom ran—
Blood that but one drop of has the worth to win
All the world forgiveness of its world of sin.

Jesu whom I look at shrouded here below,
I beseech thee send me what I thirst for so,
Some day to gaze on thee face to face in light
And be blest for ever with thy glory's sight.

From the Latin, by Gerard Manley Hopkins

Jacopone da Todi

(Ca. 1230–1306)

STABAT MATER DOLOROSA

In shade of death's sad tree
Stood doleful she.
Ah she! now by none other
Name to be known, alas, but sorrow's mother.
Before her eyes,
Hers, and the whole world's joys,
Hanging all torn she sees; and in His woes
And pains, her pangs and throes.

Each wound of His, from every part,
All, more at home in her own heart.

What kind of marble than
Is that cold man
Who can look on and see,
Nor keep such noble sorrows company?
Sure even from you
(My flints) some drops are due
To see so many unkind swords contest
So fast for one soft breast.
While with a faithful, mutual, flood,
Her eyes bleed tears, his wounds weep blood.

O costly intercourse
Of deaths and worse,
Divided loves. While son and mother
Discourse alternate wounds to one another;
Quick deaths that grow
And gather, as they come and go:
His nails write swords in her, which soon her heart
Pays back, with more than their own smart
Her swords, still growing with his pain,
Turn spears, and straight come home again.

She sees her son, her God
Bow with the load
Of borrowed sins; And swim
In woes that were not made for Him.
Ah hard command
Of Love! Here must she stand
Charg'd to look on, and with a steadfast eye
She her life die:
Leaving her only so much breath
As serves to keep alive her death.

O Mother turtle-dove!
Soft source of love

That these dry lids might borrow
Something from thy full seas of sorrow!
O in that breast
Of thine (that noblest nest
Both of love's fires and floods) might I recline
This hard, cold, heart of mine!
The chill lump would relent, and prove
Soft subject for the siege of love.

O teach those wounds to bleed
In me: me, so to read
This book of loves, thus writ
In lines of death, my life may copy it
With loyal cares.
O let me, here, claim shares;
Yield something in thy sad prerogative
(Great Queen of griefs) and give
Me too my tears: who, though all stone,
Think much that thou shouldst mourn alone.

Yea let my life and me
Fix here with thee,
And at the humble foot
Of this fair tree take our eternal root.
That so we may
At least be in love's way;
And in these chaste wars while winged wounds flee
So fast twixt Him and thee,
My breast may catch the kiss of some kind dart,
Though as at second hand, from either heart.

O you, your own best darts
Dear, doleful hearts!
Hail and strike home and make me see
That wounded bosoms their own weapons be.
Come wounds! come darts!
Nailed hands and pierced hearts!
Come your whole selves, sorrow's great son and mother!
Nor grudge a younger brother

Of griefs his portion, who (had all their due)
One single wound should not have left for you.

Shall I, set there
So deep a share
(Dear wounds) and only now
In sorrows draw no dividend with you?
O be more wise
If not more soft, mine eyes!
Flow, tardy founts! into descent showers
Dissolve my days and hours.
And if thou yet (faint soul!) defer
To bleed with Him, fail not to weep with her.

Rich Queen, lend some relief;
At least an alms of grief
To a heart who by sad right of sin
Can prove the whole sum (too sure) due to Him.
By all those stings
Of love, sweet bitter things,
Which these torn hands transcrib'd on thy true heart
O teach mine too the art
To study Him so, till we mix
Wounds; and become one crucifix.

O let me suck the wine
So long of this chaste vine
Till drunk of the dear wounds, I be
A lost thing to the world, as it to me,
O faithful friend
Of me and of my end!
Fold up my life in love; and lay't beneath
My dear Lord's vital death.
Lo, heart, thy hope's whole plea! Her precious breath
Poured out in prayers for thee; thy Lord's in death.

From the Latin, by Richard Crashaw

Dante Alighieri

(1265–1321)

From LA VITA NUOVA

Ladies that have intelligence in love,
  Of mine own lady I would speak with you;
  Not that I hope to count her praises through,
    But telling what I may, to ease my mind.
And I declare that when I speak thereof,
Love sheds such perfect sweetness over me
That if my courage failed not, certainly
    To him my listeners must be all resigned.
    Wherefore I will not speak in such large kind
That mine own speech should foil me, which were base;
But only will discourse of her high grace
    In these poor words, the best that I can find,
With you alone, dear dames and damozels:
'Twere ill to speak thereof with any else.

An angel, of his blessed knowledge, saith
  To God: "Lord, in the world that Thou has made,
  A miracle in action is displayed,
    By reason of a soul whose splendors fare
Even hither: and since Heaven requireth
  Nought saving her, for her it prayeth Thee,
  Thy saints crying aloud continually."
    Yet Pity still defends our earthly share
    In that sweet soul; God answering thus the prayer:
"My well-belovèd, suffer that in peace
Your hope remain, while so my pleasure is,
    There where one dwells who dreads the loss of her:
And who in Hell unto the doomed shall say,
'I have looked on that for which God's chosen pray.'"

My lady is desired in the high Heaven:
 Wherefore, it now behoveth me to tell,
 Saying: Let any maid that would be well
  Esteemed keep with her: for as she goes by,
Into foul hearts a deathly chill is driven
By love, that makes ill thought to perish there:
While any who endures to gaze on her
  Must either be ennobled, or else die.
  When one deserving to be raised so high
Is found, 'tis then her power attains its proof,
Making his heart strong for his soul's behoof
  With the full strength of meek humility.
Also this virtue owns she, by God's will:
Who speaks with her can never come to ill.

Love saith concerning her: "How chanceth it
 That flesh, which is of dust, should be thus pure?"
 Then, gazing always, he makes oath: "Forsure,
  This is a creature of God till now unknown."
She hath that paleness of the pearl that's fit
In a fair woman, so much and not more;
She is as high as Nature's skill can soar;
  Beauty is tried by her comparison.
  Whatever her sweet eyes are turned upon,
Spirits of love do issue thence in flame,
Which through their eyes who then may look on them
  Pierce to the heart's deep chamber every one.
And in her smile Love's image you may see;
Whence none can gaze upon her steadfastly.

Dear Song, I know thou wilt hold gentle speech
 With many ladies, when I send thee forth:
 Wherefore (being mindful that thou hadst thy birth
  From Love, and art a modest, simple child,)
Whomso thou meetest, say thou this to each:
"Give me good speed! To her I wend along
In whose much strength my weakness is made strong."
  And if, i' the end, thou wouldst not be beguiled
  Of all thy labor seek not the defiled

And common sort; but rather choose to be
Where man and woman dwell in courtesy.
        So to the road thou shalt be reconciled,
And find the Lady, and with the lady, Love.
Commend thou me to each, as doth behove.

From the Italian, by Dante G. Rossetti

THE INFERNO, CANTO XXXIV

"On march the banners of the King of Hell,"
    my Master said. "Toward us. Look straight ahead:
    can you make him out at the core of the frozen shell?"

Like a whirling windmill seen afar at twilight,
    or when a mist has risen from the ground—
    just such an engine rose upon my sight

stirring up such a wild and bitter wind
    I cowered for shelter at my Master's back,
    there being no other windbreak I could find.

I stood now where the souls of the last class
    (with fear my verses tell it) were covered wholly;
    they shone below the ice like straws in glass.

Some lie stretched out; others are fixed in place
    upright, some on their heads, some on their soles;
    another, like a bow, bends foot to face.

When we had gone so far across the ice
    that it pleased my Guide to show me the foul creature
    which once had worn the grace of Paradise,

he made me stop, and, stepping aside, he said:
    "Now see the face of Dis! This is the place
    where you must arm your soul against all dread."

Do not ask, Reader, how my blood ran cold
    and my voice choked up with fear. I cannot write it:
    this is a terror that cannot be told.

I did not die, and yet I lost life's breath:
    imagine for yourself what I became,
    deprived at once of both my life and death.

The Emperor of the Universe of Pain
    jutted his upper chest above the ice;
    and I am closer in size to the great mountain

the Titans make around the central pit,
    than they to his arms. Now, starting from this part,
    imagine the whole that corresponds to it!

If he was once as beautiful as now
    he is hideous, and still turned on his Maker,
    well may he be the source of every woe!

With what a sense of awe I saw his head
    towering above me! for it had three faces:
    one was in front, and it was fiery red;

the other two, as weirdly wonderful,
    merged with it from the middle of each shoulder
    to the point where all converged at the top of the skull;

the right was something between white and bile;
    the left was about the color that one finds
    on those who live along the banks of the Nile.

Under each head two wings rose terribly,
    their span proportioned to so gross a bird:
    I never saw such sails upon the sea.

They were not feathers—their texture and their form
    were like a bat's wings—and he beat them so
    that three winds blew from him in one great storm:

it is these winds that freeze all Cocytus.
    He wept from his six eyes, and down three chins
    the tears ran mixed with bloody froth and pus.

In every mouth he worked a broken sinner
    between his rake-like teeth. Thus he kept three
    in eternal pain at his eternal dinner.

For the one in front the biting seemed to play
    no part at all compared to the ripping: at times
    the whole skin of his back was flayed away.

"That soul that suffers most," explained my Guide,
    "is Judas Iscariot, he who kicks his legs
    on the fiery chin and has his head inside.

Of the other two, who have their heads thrust forward,
    the one who dangles down from the black face
    is Brutus: note how he writhes without a word.

And there, with the huge and sinewy arms, is the soul
    of Cassius.—But the night is coming on
    and we must go, for we have seen the whole."

Then, as he bade, I clasped his neck, and he,
    watching for a moment when the wings
    were opened wide, reached over dexterously

and seized the shaggy coat of the king demon;
    then grappling matted hair and frozen crusts
    from one tuft to another, clambered down.

When we had reached the joint where the great thigh
    merges into the swelling of the haunch,
    my Guide and Master, straining terribly,

turned his head to where his feet had been
    and began to grip the hair as if he were climbing;
    so that I thought we moved toward Hell again.

"Hold fast!" my Guide said, and his breath came shrill
    with labor and exhaustion. "There is no way
    but by such stairs to rise above such evil."

At last he climbed out through an opening
    in the central rock, and he seated me on the rim;
    then joined me with a nimble backward spring.

I looked up, thinking to see Lucifer
    as I had left him, and I saw instead
    his legs projecting high into the air.

44

Now let all those whose dull minds are still vexed
    by failure to understand what point it was
    I had passed through, judge if I was perplexed.

"Get up. Up on your feet," my Master said.
    "The sun already mounts to middle tierce,
    and a long road and hard climbing lie ahead."

It was no hall of state we had found there,
    but a natural animal pit hollowed from rock
    with a broken floor and a close and sunless air.

"Before I tear myself from the Abyss,"
    I said when I had risen, "O my Master,
    explain to me my error in all this:

where is the ice? and Lucifer—how has he been turned fro
    been turned from top to bottom: and how can the sun
    have gone from night to day so suddenly?"

And he to me: "You imagine you are still
    on the other side of the center where I grasped
    the shaggy flank of the Great Worm of Evil

which bores through the world—you *were* while I climbed down,
    but when I turned myself about, you passed
    the point to which all gravities are drawn.

You are under the other hemisphere where you stand;
    the sky above us is the half opposed
    to that which canopies the great dry land.

Under the mid-point of that other sky
    the Man who was born sinless and who lived
    beyond a blemish, came to suffer and die.

You have your feet upon a little sphere
    which forms the other face of the Judecca.
    There it is evening when it is morning here.

And this gross Fiend and Image of all Evil
    who made a stairway for us with his hide
    is pinched and prisoned in the ice-pack still.

On this side he plunged down from heaven's height,
   and the land that spread here once hid in the sea
   and fled North to our hemisphere for fright;

and it may be that moved by that same fear,
   the one peak that still rises on this side
   fled upward leaving this great cavern here.

Down there, beginning at the further bound
   of Beelzebub's dim tomb, there is a space
   not known by sight, but only by the sound

or a little stream descending through the hollow
   it has eroded from the massive stone
   in its endlessly entwining lazy flow."

My Guide and I crossed over and began
   to mount that little known and lightless road
   to ascend into the shining world again.

He first, I second, without thought of rest
   we climbed the dark until we reached the point
   where a round opening brought in sight the blest

and beauteous shining of the Heavenly cars.
And we walked out once more beneath the Stars.

From the Italian, by John Ciardi

PURGATORY, CANTO XXVI

So, one before the other, we moved there
   along the edge, and my Sweet Guide kept saying:
   "Walk only where you see me walk. Take care."

The Sun, already changing from blue to white
   the face of the western sky, struck at my shoulder,
   its rays now almost level on my right;

and my shadow made the flames a darker red.
   Even so slight an evidence, I noticed,
   made many shades that walked there turn their head.

And when they saw my shadow, these began
    to speak of me, saying to one another:
    "He seems to be no shade, but a living man!"

And some of them drew near me then—as near
    as they could come, for they were ever careful
    to stay within the fire that burned them there.

"O you who trail the others—with no desire
    to lag, I think, but out of deference—
    speak to me who am burned by thirst and fire.

Not I alone need what your lips can tell:
    all these thirst for it more than Ethiopes
    or Indians for a drink from a cold well:

how is it that you cast a shadow yet,
    making yourself a barrier to the Sun,
    as if death had not caught you in its net?"

—So one addressed me. And I should have been
    explaining myself already, but for a new
    surprising sight that caught my eye just then;

for down the center of that fiery way
    came new souls from the opposite direction,
    and I forgot what I had meant to say.

I saw them hurrying from either side,
    and each shade kissed another, without pausing,
    each by the briefest greeting satisfied.

(Ants, in their dark ranks, meet exactly so,
    rubbing each other's noses, to ask perhaps
    what luck they've had, or which way they should go.)

As soon as they break off their friendly greeting,
    before they take the first step to pass on,
    each shade outshouts the other at that meeting.

"Sodom and Gomorrah," the new souls cry.
    And the others: "Pasiphaë enters the cow
    to call the young bull to her lechery."

As if cranes split into two flocks, and one
    flew to the Rhipheans, one to the sands,
    these to escape the ice, and those the Sun—

so, then, those shades went their opposing ways;
    and all returned in tears to their first song,
    and each to crying an appropriate praise.

Then those who came my way drew close once more—
    the same shades that had first entreated me.
    They seemed as eager to hear me as before.

I, having had their wish presented twice,
    replied without delay: "O souls assured—
    whenever it may be—of Paradise,

I did not leave my limbs beyond the flood,
    not green nor ripe, but bear them with me here
    in their own jointure and in their own blood.

I go to be no longer blind. Above
    there is a lady wins us grace, and I,
    still mortal, cross your world led by her love.

But now I pray—so may it soon befall
    you have your greater wish to be called home
    into that heaven of love that circles all—

tell me, that I may write down what you say
    for all to read, who are you? and those others
    who move away behind you—who are they?"

Just as our mountaineers, their first time down,
    half-wild and shaggy, gape about the streets
    and stare in dumb amazement at the town—

just such a look I saw upon those shades;
    but when they had recovered from their stupor
    (which from a lofty heart the sooner fades),

the first shade spoke again: "Blessèd are you
    who for a better life, store in your soul
    experience of these realms you travel through!

Those souls you saw going the other way
    grew stained in that for which triumphant Caesar
    heard his own legions call him 'Queen' one day.

Therefore their band, at parting from us, cries
    'Sodom!'—as you have heard—that by their shame
    they aid the fire that makes them fit to rise.

We were hermaphroditic in our offenses,
    but since we did not honor human laws,
    yielding like animals to our lusting senses,

we, when we leave the other band, repent
    by crying to our shame the name of her
    who crouched in the mock-beast with beast's intent.

And now you know our actions and our crime.
    But if you wish our names, we are so many
    I do not know them all, nor is there time.

Your wish to know mine shall be satisfied:
    I am Guido Guinizelli, here so soon
    because I repented fully before I died."

In King Lycurgus' darkest hour, two sons
    discovered their lost mother: I was moved
    as they had been (but could not match their actions)

when I heard his name, for he had fathered me
    and all the rest, my betters, who have sung
    sweet lilting rhymes of love and courtesy.

Enraptured, I can neither speak nor hear
    but only stare at him as we move on,
    although the flames prevent my drawing near.

When at last my eyes had fed, I spoke anew;
and in such terms as win belief, I offered
to serve him in whatever I could do.

And he to me then: "What you say has made
such a profound impression on my mind
as Lethe cannot wash away, nor fade.

But if the words you swore just now are true,
let me know why you show by word and look
such love as I believe I see in you?"

And I to him: "Your songs so sweet and clear
which, for as long as modern usage lives,
shall make the very ink that writes them dear."

"Brother," he said, "that one who moves along
ahead there," (and he pointed) "was in life
a greater craftsman of the mother tongue.

He, in his love songs and his tales in prose,
was without peer—and if fools claim Limoges
produced a better, there are always those

who measure worth by popular acclaim,
ignoring principles of art and reason
to base their judgments on the author's name.

So, once, our fathers sent Guittone's praise,
and his alone, bounding from cry to cry,
though truth prevails with most men nowadays.

And now, if you enjoy such privilege
that you are free to go up to that cloister
within which Christ is abbot of the college,

say an Our Father for me in that host,
as far as it may serve us in this world
in which the very power to sin is lost."

With that, perhaps to yield his place with me
    to someone else he vanished through the fire
    as a fish does to the dark depths of the sea.

I drew ahead till I was by that shade
    he had pointed to, and said that in my heart
    a grateful place to feast his name was laid.

And he replied at once and willingly:
    "Such pleasaunce have I of thy gentilesse,
    that I ne can, ne will I hide from thee.

Arnaut am I, and weepe and sing my faring.
    In grievousnesse I see my follies past;
    in joie, the blistful daie of my preparing.

And by that eke virtue, I thee implour,
    that redeth thee, that thou amount the staire,
    be mindful in thy time of my dolour."

Then he, too, hid himself within the fire
that makes those spirits ready to go higher.

From the Italian, by John Ciardi

PARADISE, CANTO XXXIII

"Virgin Mother, daughter of thy son;
    humble beyond all creatures and more exalted;
    predestined turning point of God's intention;

thy merit so ennobled human nature
    that its divine Creator did not scorn
    to make Himself the creature of His own creature.

The Love that was rekindled in Thy womb
    sends forth the warmth of the eternal peace
    within whose ray this flower has come to bloom.

Here, to us, thou art the noon and scope
of Love revealed; and among mortal men,
the living fountain of eternal hope.

Lady, thou art so near God's reckonings
that who seeks grace and does not first seek thee
would have his wish fly upward without wings.

Not only does thy sweet benignity
flow out to all who beg, but oftentimes
thy charity arrives before the plea.

In thee is pity, in thee munificence,
in thee the tenderest heart, in thee unites
all that creation knows of excellence!

Now comes this man who from the final pit
of the universe up to this height has seen,
one by one, the three lives of the spirit.

He prays to thee in fervent supplication
for grace and strength, that he may raise his eyes
to the all-healing final revelation.

And I, who never more desired to see
the vision myself than I do that he may see It,
add my own prayer, and pray that it may be

enough to move you to dispel the trace
of every mortal shadow by thy prayers
and let him see revealed the Sum of Grace.

I pray thee further, all-persuading Queen,
keep whole the natural bent of his affections
and of his powers after his eyes have seen.

Protect him from the stirrings of man's clay;
see how Beatrice and the blessed host
clasp reverent hands to join me as I pray."

The eyes that God reveres and loves the best
   glowed on the speaker, making clear the joy
   with which true prayer is heard by the most blest.

Those eyes turned then to the Eternal Ray,
   through which, we must indeed believe, the eyes
   of others do not find such ready way.

And I, who neared the goal of all my nature,
   felt my soul, at the climax of its yearning,
   suddenly, as it ought, grow calm with rapture.

Bernard then, smiling sweetly, gestured to me
   to look up, but I had already become
   within myself all he would have me be.

Little by little as my vision grew
   it penetrated further through the aura
   of the high lamp which in Itself is true.

What then I saw is more than tongue can say.
   Our human speech is dark before the vision.
   The ravished memory swoons and falls away.

As one who sees in dreams and wakes to find
   the emotional impression of his vision
   still powerful while its parts fade from his mind—

just such am I, having lost nearly all
   the vision itself, while in my heart I feel
   the sweetness of it yet distill and fall.

So, in the sun, the footprints fade from snow.
   On the wild wind that bore the tumbling leaves
   the Sybil's oracles were scattered so.

O Light Supreme who doth Thyself withdraw
   so far above man's mortal understanding,
   lend me again some glimpse of what I saw;

make Thou my tongue so eloquent it may
    of all Thy glory speak a single clue
    to those who follow me in the world's day;

for by returning to my memory
    somewhat, and somewhat sounding in these verses,
    Thou shalt show man more of Thy victory.

So dazzling was the splendor of that Ray,
    that I must certainly have lost my senses
    had I, but for an instant, turned away.

And so it was, as I recall, I could
    the better bear to look, until at last
    my vision made one with the Eternal Good.

Oh grace abounding that had made me fit
    to fix my eyes on the eternal light
    until my vision was consumed in it!

I saw within Its depth how It conceives
    all things in a single volume bound by Love,
    of which the universe is the scattered leaves;

substance, accident, and their relation
    so fused that all I say could do no more
    than yield a glimpse of that bright revelation.

I think I saw the universal form
    that binds these things, for as I speak these words
    I feel my joy swell and my spirits warm.

Twenty-five centuries since Neptune saw
    the Argo's keel have not moved all mankind,
    recalling that adventure, to such awe

as I felt in an instant. My tranced being
    stared fixed and motionless upon that vision,
    ever more fervent to see in the act of seeing.

Experiencing that Radiance, the spirit
    is so indrawn it is impossible
    even to think of ever turning from It.

For the good which is the will's ultimate object
    is all subsumed in It; and, being removed,
    all is defective which in It is perfect.

Now in my recollection of the rest
    I have less power to speak than any infant
    wetting its tongue yet at its mother's breast;

and not because that Living Radiance bore
    more than one semblance, for It is unchanging
    and is forever as it was before;

rather, as I grew worthier to see,
    the more I looked, the more unchanging semblance
    appeared to change with every change in me.

Within the depthless deep and clear existence
    of that abyss of light three circles shown—
    three in color, one in circumference:

the second from the first, rainbow from rainbow;
    the third, an exhalation of pure fire
    equally breathed forth by the other two.

But oh how much my words miss my conception,
    which is itself so far from what I saw
    that to call it feeble would be rank deception!

O Light Eternal fixed in Itself alone,
    by Itself alone understood, which from Itself
    loves and glows, self-knowing and self-known;

that second aureole which shone forth in Thee,
    conceived as a reflection of the first—
    or which appeared so to my scrutiny—

seemed in Itself of Its own coloration
    to be painted with man's image. I fixed my eyes
    on that alone in rapturous contemplation.

Like a geometer wholly dedicated
    to squaring the circle, but who cannot find,
    think as he may, the principle indicated—

so did I study the supernal face.
    I yearned to know just how our image merges
    into that circle, and how it there finds place;

but mine were not the wings for such a flight.
    Yet, as I wished, the truth I wished for came
    cleaving my mind in a great flash of light.

Here my powers rest from their high fantasy,
    but already I could feel my being turned—
    instinct and intellect balanced equally

as in a wheel whose motion nothing jars—
by the Love that moves the Sun and the other stars.

From the Italian, by John Ciardi

Juan Ruiz of Hita

(Ca. 1283–ca. 1350)

HYMN TO THE VIRGIN

Thou Flower of flowers! I'll follow thee,
And sing thy praise unweariedly:
Best of the best! O, may I ne'er
From thy pure service flee!

Lady, to thee I turn my eyes,
On thee my trusting hope relies;
O, let thy spirit, smiling here,
Chase my anxieties!

Most Holy Virgin! tired and faint,
I pour my melancholy plaint;
Yet lift a tremulous thought to thee,
Alas, 'midst mortal taint.

Thou Ocean-Star! thou Port of joy!
From pain, and sadness, and annoy,

O, rescue me, O, comfort me,
Bright Lady of the Sky!

Thy mercy is a boundless mine;
Freedom from care, and life are thine;
He recks not, faints not, fears not, who
Trusts in thy power divine.

Unjustly I do suffer wrong,
Despair and darkness guide my song;
I see no other, come, do thou
Waft my weak bark along!

From the Spanish, by Henry W. Longfellow

Anonymous

(Ca. thirteenth century)

THE ELECTED KNIGHT

Sir Oluf he rideth over the plain,
    Full seven miles broad and seven miles wide,
But never, ah never can meet with the man
    A tilt with him dare ride.

He saw under the hillside
    A Knight full well equipped;
His steed was black, his helm was barred;
    He was riding at full speed.

He wore upon his spurs
    Twelve little golden birds;
Anon he spurred his steed with a clang,
    And there sat all the birds and sang.

He wore upon his spurs
    Twelve little golden wheels;
Anon in eddies the wild wind blew,
    And round and round the wheels they flew.

He wore upon his helm,
   A wreath of ruddy gold;
And that gave him the Maidens three.
   The youngest was fair to behold.

Sir Oluf questioned the Knight eftsoon
   If he were come from heaven down;
"Art thou Christ of Heaven," quote he,
   "So will I yield me unto thee."

"I am not Christ the Great,
   Thou shalt not yield thee yet;
I am an Unknown Knight,
   Three modest Maidens have me bedight."

"Art thou a Knight elected,
   And have three Maidens thee bedight;
So shalt thou ride a tilt this day,
   For all the Maidens' honor!"

The first tilt they together rode
   They put their steeds to the test;
The second tilt they together rode,
   They proved their manhood best.

The third tilt they together rode,
   Neither of them would yield;
The fourth tilt they together rode,
   They both fell on the field.

Now lie the lords upon the plain,
   And their blood runs unto death;
Now sit the Maidens in the high tower,
   The youngest sorrows till death.

From the Danish, by Henry W. Longfellow

Anonymous

(Ca. thirteenth century)

CONTAKION OF THE DEPARTED

Give rest, O Christ,
    to thy servant with thy saints:
    where sorrow and pain are no more;
    neither sighing, but life everlasting.
Thou only art immortal,
    the Creator and Maker of man:
    and we are mortal, formed of the earth,
    and unto earth shall we return:
    for so thou didst ordain,
    when thou createdst me, saying,
    "Dust thou art, and unto dust shalt thou return."
All we go down to the dust;
    and weeping over the grave,
    we make our song:
    alleluya, alleluya, alleluya.
Give rest, O Christ,
    to thy servant with thy saints,
    where sorrow and pain are no more;
    neither sighing, but life everlasting.

Anonymous translation from the Russian

Richard Rolle

(1290–1349)

LOVE IS LIFE

For now, love thou, I rede, Christ, as I thee tell:
And with Angels take thy stead; that joy look thou nought sell!
In earth thou hate, I rede, all that thy love may fell:
For Love is stalworth as the death, Love is hard as hell.

Love is a light burden, Love gladdeth young and old;
Love is without pine, as lovers have me told:
Love is a ghostly wine, that makes men big and bold:
Of Love shall he nothing tyne that it in heart will hold.

But fleshly love shall fare as doth the flower in May
And lasting be no more than one hour of a day,
And sithen sigh full sore their lust, their pride, their play,
When they are cast in care, till pine that lasteth aye.

Jesu is Love that lasteth aye: to Him is our longing:
Jesu is night turneth to day, the dawning into spring.
Jesu, think on us now and aye: for Thee we hold our King:
Jesu, give us grace, as Thou well may, to love Thee without ending.

William Langland

(1332–1395)

From PIERS PLOWMAN

But beggars about midsummer go beardless to supper,
And winter is yet worse, for they are wet-shod wanderers,
Frozen and famished and foully challenged
And berated by rich men so that it is rueful to listen.

Now Lord, send them summer or some manner of happiness
After their going hence for what they have here suffered.
For thou mightest have made us equal, none meaner than another,
With equal wit and wisdom, if such had been thy wishes.
Have ruth on these rich men who reward not thy prisoners,
Many are *ingrati* of the good that thou hast given them.
But God, in thy goodness, grant them grace of amendment.
For they dread not dearth nor drought nor freshets,
Nor heat nor hail, if they have their comfort.
Nothing is wanting to them here of what they wish and will.

But poor people, thy prisoners, Lord, in the pit of misery,
Comfort thy creatures who have such care to suffer
Through dearth, through drought, all their days here.
Woe in winter for want of clothing!
Who seldom in summer-time sup fully!

Anonymous translation from the Middle English

Geoffrey Chaucer

(1340–1400)

THE CANTERBURY TALES: From the Prologue

When in April the sweet showers fall
And pierce the drought of March to the root, and all
The veins are bathed in liquor of such power
As brings about the engendering of the flower,
When also Zephyrus with his sweet breath
Exhales an air in every grove and heath
Upon the tender shoots, and the young sun
His half-course in the sign of the *Ram* has run,
And the small fowl are making melody
That sleep away the night with open eye
(So nature pricks them and their heart engages)
Then people long to go on pilgrimages

And palmers long to seek the stranger strands
Of far-off saints, hallowed in sundry lands,
And specially, from every shire's end
In England, down to Canterbury they wend
To seek the holy blissful martyr, quick
To give his help to them when they were sick.

It happened in that season that one day
In Southwark, at *The Tabard*, as I lay
Ready to go on pilgrimage and start
For Canterbury, most devout at heart,
At night there came into that hostelry
Some nine and twenty in a company
Of sundry folk happening then to fall
In fellowship, and they were pilgrims all
That towards Canterbury meant to ride.
The rooms and stables of the inn were wide;
They made us easy, all was of the best.
And shortly, when the sun had gone to rest,
By speaking to them all upon the trip
I soon was one of them in fellowship
And promised to rise early and take the way
To Canterbury, as you heard me say.

But none the less, while I have time and space,
Before my story takes a further pace,
It seems a reasonable thing to say
What their condition was, the full array
Of each of them, as it appeared to me
According to profession and degree,
And what apparel they were riding in;
And at a Knight I therefore will begin.
There was a *Knight*, a most distinguished man,
Who from the day on which he first began
To ride abroad had followed chivalry,
Truth, honour, generousness and courtesy.
He had done nobly in his sovereign's war
And ridden into battle, no man more,
As well in christian as in heathen places,
And ever honoured for his noble graces.

When we took Alexandria, he was there.
He often sat at table in the chair
Of honour, above all nations, when in Prussia.
In Lithuania he had ridden, and Russia,
No christian man so often, of his rank.
When, in Granada, Algeciras sank
Under assault, he had been there, and in
North Africa, raiding Benamarin;
In Anatolia he had been as well
And fought when Ayas and Attalia fell,
For all along the Mediterranean coast
He had embarked with many a noble host.
In fifteen mortal battles he had been
And jousted for our faith at Tramissene
Thrice in the lists, and always killed his man.
This same distinguished knight had led the van
Once with the Bey of Balat, doing work
For him against another heathen Turk;
He was of sovereign value in all eyes.
And though so much distinguished, he was wise
And in his bearing modest as a maid.
He never yet a boorish thing had said
In all his life to any, come what might;
He was a true, a perfect gentle-knight.

. . . .

There also was a *Nun*, a Prioress,
Her way of smiling very simple and coy.
Her greatest oath was only 'By St Loy!'
And she was known as Madam Eglantyne.
And well she sang a service, with a fine
Intoning through her nose, as was most seemly,
And she spoke daintily in French, extremely,
After the school of Stratford-atte-Bowe;
French in the Paris style she did not know.
At meat her manners were well taught withal;
No morsel from her lips did she let fall,
Nor dipped her fingers in the sauce too deep;
But she could carry a morsel up and keep

The smallest drop from falling on her breast.
For courtliness she had a special zest,
And she would wipe her upper lip so clean
That not a trace of grease was to be seen
Upon the cup when she had drunk; to eat,
She reached a hand sedately for the meat.
She certainly was very entertaining,
Pleasant and friendly in her ways, and straining
To counterfeit a courtly kind of grace,
A stately bearing fitting to her place,
And to seem dignified in all her dealings.
As for her sympathies and tender feelings,
She was so charitably solicitous
She used to weep if she but saw a mouse
Caught in a trap, if it were dead or bleeding.
And she had little dogs she would be feeding
With roasted flesh, or milk, or fine white bread.
And bitterly she wept if one were dead
Or someone took a stick and made it smart;
She was all sentiment and tender heart.
Her veil was gathered in a seemly way,
Her nose was elegant, her eyes glass-grey;
Her mouth was very small, but soft and red,
Her forehead, certainly was fair of spread,
Almost a span across the brows, I own;
She was indeed by no means undergrown.
Her cloak, I noticed, had a graceful charm.
She wore a coral trinket on her arm,
A set of beads, the gaudies tricked in green,
Whence hung a golden brooch of brightest sheen
On which there first was graven a crowned A,
And lower, *Amor vincit omnia*.

. . . .

   A worthy *woman* from beside *Bath* city
Was with us, somewhat deaf, which was a pity.
In making cloth she showed so great a bent
She bettered those of Ypres and of Ghent.
In all the parish not a dame dared stir

Towards the altar steps in front of her,
And if indeed they did, so wrath was she
As to be quite put out of charity.
Her kerchiefs were of finely woven ground;
I dared have sworn they weighed a good ten pound,
The ones she wore on Sunday, on her head.
Her hose were of the finest scarlet red
And gartered tight; her shoes were soft and new.
Bold was her face, handsome, and red in hue.
A worthy woman all her life, what's more
She'd had five husbands, all at the church door,
Apart from other company in youth;
No need just now to speak of that, forsooth.
And she had thrice been to Jerusalem,
Seen many strange rivers and passed over them;
She'd been to Rome and also to Boulogne,
St James of Compostella and Cologne,
And she was skilled in wandering by the way.
She had gap-teeth, set widely, truth to say.
Easily on an ambling horse she sat
Well wimpled up, and on her head a hat
As broad as is a buckler or a shield;
She had a flowing mantle that concealed
Large hips, her heels spurred sharply under that.
In company she liked to laugh and chat
And knew the remedies for love's mischances,
An art in which she knew the oldest dances.

   A holy-minded man of good renown
There was, and poor, the *Parson* to a town,
Yet he was rich in holy thought and work.
He also was a learned man, a clerk,
Who truly knew Christ's gospel and would preach it
Devoutly to parishioners, and teach it.
Benign and wonderfully diligent,
And patient when adversity was sent
(For so he proved in great adversity)
He much disliked extorting tithe or fee,
Nay rather he preferred beyond a doubt

Giving to poor parishioners round about
From his own goods and Easter offerings.
He found sufficiency in little things.
Wide was his parish, with houses far asunder,
Yet he neglected not in rain or thunder,
In sickness or in grief, to pay a call
On the remotest, whether great or small,
Upon his feet, and in his hand a stave.
This noble example to his sheep he gave,
First following the word before he taught it,
And it was from the gospel he had caught it.
This little proverb he would add thereto
That if gold rust, what then will iron do?
For if a priest be foul in whom we trust
No wonder that a common man should rust;
And shame it is to see—let priests take stock—
A shitten shepherd and a snowy flock.
The true example that a priest should give
Is one of cleanness, how the sheep should live.
He did not set his benefice to hire
And leave his sheep encumbered in the mire
Or run to London to earn easy bread
By singing masses for the wealthy dead,
Or find some Brotherhood and get enrolled.
He stayed at home and watched over his fold
So that no wolf should make the sheep miscarry.
He was a shepherd and no mercenary.
Holy and virtuous he was, but then
Never contemptuous of sinful men,
Never disdainful, never too proud or fine,
But was discreet in teaching and benign.
His business was to show a fair behaviour
And draw men thus to Heaven and their Saviour,
Unless indeed a man were obstinate;
And such, whether of high or low estate,
He put to sharp rebuke to say the least.
I think there never was a better priest.
He sought no pomp or glory in his dealings,

No scrupulosity had spiced his feelings.
Christ and His Twelve Apostles and their lore
He taught, but followed it himself before.

There was a *Plowman* with him there, his brother
Many a load of dung one time or other
He must have carted through the morning dew.
He was an honest worker, good and true,
Living in peace and perfect charity,
And, as the gospel bade him, so did he,
Loving God best with all his heart and mind
And then his neighbour as himself, repined
At no misfortune, slacked for no content,
For steadily about his work he went
To thrash his corn, to dig or to manure
Or make a ditch; and he would help the poor
For love of Christ and never take a penny
If he could help it, and, as prompt as any,
He paid his tithes in full when they were due
On what he owned, and on his earnings too.
He wore a tabard smock and rode a mare.

. . . .

There was a *Summoner* with us in the place
Who had a fire-red cherubinnish face,
For he had carbuncles. His eyes were narrow,
He was as hot and lecherous as a sparrow.
Black, scabby brows he had, and a thin beard.
Children were afraid when he appeared.
No quicksilver, lead ointments, tartar creams,
Boracic, no, nor brimstone, so it seems,
Could make a salve that had the power to bite,
Clean up or cure his whelks of knobby white
Or purge the pimples sitting on his cheeks.
Garlic he loved, and onions too, and leeks,
And drinking strong red wine till all was hazy.
Then he would shout and jabber as if crazy,
And wouldn't speak a word except in Latin
When he was drunk, such tags as he was pat in;
He only had a few, say two or three,

67

That he had mugged up out of some decree;
No wonder, for he heard them every day.
And, as you know, a man can teach a jay
To call out 'Walter' better than the Pope.
But had you tried to test his wits and grope
For more, You'd have found nothing in the bag.
Then *'Questio quid juris'* was his tag.
He was a gentle varlet and a kind one,
No better fellow if you went to find one.
He would allow—just for a quart of wine—
Any good lad to keep a concubine
A twelvemonth and dispense it altogether!
Yet he could pluck a finch to leave no feather:
And if he found some rascal with a maid
He would instruct him not to be afraid
In such a case of the Archdeacon's curse
(Unless the rascal's soul were in his purse)
For in his purse the punishment should be.
'Purse is the good Archdeacon's Hell,' said he.
But well I know he lied in what he said;
A curse should put a guilty man in dread,
For curses kill, as shriving brings, salvation.
We should beware of excommunication.
Thus, as he pleased, the man could bring duress
On any young fellow in the diocese.
He knew their secrets, they did what he said.
He wore a garland set upon his head
Large as the holly-bush upon a stake
Outside an ale-house, and he had a cake,
A round one, which it was his joke to wield
As if it were intended for a shield.

    He and a gentle *Pardoner* rode together,
A bird from Charing Cross of the same feather,
Just back from visiting the Court of Rome.
He loudly sang *'Come hither, love, come home!'*
The Summoner sang deep seconds to this song,
No trumpet ever sounded half so strong.

This Pardoner had hair as yellow as wax,
Hanging down smoothly like a hank of flax.
In driblets fell his locks behind his head
Down to his shoulders which they overspread;
Thinly they fell, like rat-tails, one by one.
He wore no hood upon his head, for fun;
The hood inside his wallet had been stowed,
He aimed at riding in the latest mode;
But for a little cap his head was bare
And he had bulging eye-balls, like a hare.
He'd sewed a holy relic on his cap;
His wallet lay before him on his lap,
Brimful of pardons come from Rome all hot.
He had the same small voice a goat has got.
His chin no beard had harboured, nor would harbour,
Smoother than ever chin was left by barber.
I judge he was a gelding, or a mare.
As to his trade, from Berwick down to Ware
There was no pardoner of equal grace,
For in his trunk he had a pillow-case
Which he asserted was Our Lady's veil.
He said he had a gobbet of the sail
Saint Peter had the time when he made bold
To walk the waves, till Jesu Christ took hold.
He had a cross of metal set with stones
And, in a glass, a rubble of pigs' bones.
And with these relics, any time he found
Some poor up-country parson to astound,
On one short day, in money down, he drew
More than the parson in a month or two,
And by his flatteries and prevarication
Made monkeys of the priest and congregation.
But still to do him justice first and last
In church he was a noble ecclesiast.
How well he read a lesson or told a story!
But best of all he sang an Offertory,
For well he knew that when that song was sung

He'd have to preach and tune his honey-tongue
And (well he could) win silver from the crowd.
That's why he sang so merrily and loud.

From the Middle English, by Nevill Coghill

Bernard Rascas

(D.1353)

THE LOVE OF GOD

All things that are on earth shall wholly pass away,
Except the love of God, which shall live and last for aye.
The forms of men shall be as they had never been;
The blasted groves shall lose their fresh and tender green;
The birds of the thicket shall end their pleasant song,
And the nightingale shall cease to chant the evening long.
The kine of pasture shall feel the dart that kills,
And all the fair white flocks shall perish from the hills.
The goat and antlered stag, the wolf and the fox,
The wild boar of the wood, and the chamois of the rocks,
And the strong and fearless bear, in the trodden dust shall lie;
And the dolphin of the sea, and the mightly whale shall die.
And realms shall be dissolved, and empires be no more,
And they shall bow to death, who rules from shore to shore;
And the great globe itself, so Holy Writings tell,
With the rolling firmament, where starry armies dwell,
Shall melt with fervent heat,—they shall all pass away,
Except the love of God, which shall live and last for aye!

From the Portuguese, by William Cullen Bryant

John Lygate

(1370–1451)

TO THE VIRGIN

Queen of Heaven, of Hell eke Emperess,
Lady of this world, O very lodestar!
To mariners gainst all mortal distress
In their passage that they do not err;
Thy look of mercy cast down from so far
On all thy servants by chaste compassion,
Grant them good peace, save them from mortal war,
To thy five Joys that have devotion.

Celestial Cypress set upon Syon,
Highest Cedar of perfit holiness,
Carbuncle of charity and green emerald stone,
Whole and unbroken by virginal clearness;
O sapphire, loupe all swelling to repress
On cankered sores and venomous feloun,
In ghostly woundes by their governess,
To thy five Joys that have devotion.

Yard of Aaron, gracious and benign,
Well of all grace and merciful pity,
Where the Holy Ghost list to close and sign
The crystal cloister of thy Virginity;
Balm of Engadi gainst all Infirmity,
Of folk that languish to tribulation,
Perserve and keep from all adversity,
To thy five Joys that have devotion.

As dew in Aprille
    That fallith on the gras.

He cam also stille
    To his moderes bowr,
As dew in Aprille
    That fallith on the flowr.

He cam also stille
    Ther his moder lay,
As dew in Aprille
    That fallith on the spray.

Moder and maiden
    Was never non but che;
Wel may swich a lady
    Godes moder be.

John Skelton

(1460?–1529)

UPON A DEAD MAN'S HEAD

Your ugly token
My mind hath broken
From worldly lust:
For I have discust
We are but dust,
And die we must.
  It is general
To be mortal:
I have well espied
No man may him hide
From Death hollow-eyed,
With sinews wyderéd,
With bones shyderéd,
With his worm-eaten maw,
And his ghastly jaw

Gasping aside,
Naked of hide,
Neither flesh nor fell.
    Then, by my counsel,
Look that ye spell
Well this gospel:
For whereso we dwell
Death will us quell,
And with us mell.
    For all our pampered paunches
There may no fraunchis,
Nor wordly bliss,
Redeem us from this:
Our days be dated
To be checkmated
With draughtēs of death
Stopping our breath:
Our eyen sinking,
Our bodies stinking,
Our gummēs grinning,
Our soulēs brinning.
To whom, then, shall we sue,
For to have rescue,
But to sweet Jesu
On us then for to rue?
    O goodly Child
Of Mary mild,
Then be our shield!
That we be not exiled
To the dyne dale
Of bootless bale,
Nor to the lake
Of fiendēs black.
    But grant us grace
To see thy Face,
And to purcháse
Thine heavenly place,
And thy paláce

Full of soláce
Above the sky
That is so high;
Eternally
To behold and see
The Trinity!
    Amen.

part three

Renaissance Christian Poems

"Love, lift me up upon thy golden wings. . . ."

The lion is a symbol of the Resurrection and of the Gospel According to Mark. When used as a Resurrection symbol it refers to the belief once held that lion cubs are born dead and given life three days after their birth by the breath of their sire.

Francesco Petrarch

(1304–1374)

FATHER IN HEAVEN! AFTER THE DAYS MISSPENT

Father in heaven! after the days misspent
   After the nights of wild tumultuous thought,
In that fierce passion's strong entanglement
   One, for my peace too lovely far, had wrought;
Vouchsafe that by Thy grace, my spirit bent
   On nobler aims, to holier ways be brought;
That so my foe, spreading with dark intent
   His mortal snares, be foiled, and held at nought.

E'en now the eleventh year its course fulfils,
   That I have bowed me to the tyranny
      Relentless most to fealty most tried.
Have mercy, Lord! on my unworthy ills;
   Fix all my thoughts in contemplation high;
      How on the Cross this day a Saviour died.

From the Italian, by Barberina Dacre

ON THE DEATH OF THE LADY LAURA

In thought I raised me to the place where she
   Whom still on earth I seek and find not, shines;
   There mid the souls whom the third sphere confines,
   More fair I found her and less proud to me.
She took my hand and said: Here shalt thou be
   With me ensphered, unless desires mislead;

79

Lo! I am she who made thy bosom bleed,
Whose day ere eve was ended utterly:
My bliss no mortal heart can understand;
    Thee only do I lack, and that which thou
    So loved, now left on earth, my beauteous veil.
Ah! wherefore did she cease and loose my hand?
    For at the sound of that celestial tale
    I all but stayed in paradise till now.

From the Italian, by John Addington Symonds

AGAINST THE COURT OF ROME

Vengeance must fall on thee, thou filthy whore
Of Babylon, thou breaker of Christ's fold,
That from acorns, and from the water cold,
Art rich become with making many poor
Thou treason's nest that in thy heart dost hold
Of cankard malice, and of mischief more
Than pen can write, or may with tongue be told,
Slave to delights that chastity hath sold;
For wine and ease which setteth all thy store
Upon whoredome and none other lore,
In thy palace of strumpets young and old
There walks Plenty and Belzebub thy Lord:
Guides thee and them, and doth thy reign uphold:
It is but late, as writing will record,
That poor thou wert withouten land or gold;
Yet now hath gold and pride, by one accord,
In wickedness so spread thy life abroad,
That it doth stink before the face of God.

From the Italian, by Thomas Wyatt

Girolamo Benieveni

(1453–1542)

LAUDA

Jesus, whoso with Thee
Hangs not in pain and loss,
Pierced on the cruel cross,
　At peace shall never be.
Lord, unto me be kind;
Give me that peace of mind
Which in this world so blind
　And false, dwells but with Thee.
Give me that strife and pain,
Apart from which 'twere vain
Thy love on earth to gain
　Or seek a share with Thee.
If, Lord, with Thee alone
Heart's peace and love be known,
My heart shall be Thine own,
　Ever to rest with Thee.
Here in my heart be lit
Thy fire, to feed on it,
Till, burning bit by bit
　It dies to live with Thee.
　Jesus, whoso with Thee
Hangs not in pain and loss,
Pierced on the cruel cross,
　At peace shall never be.

From the Italian, by John Addington Symonds

Giovanni Pico Della Mirandola
(1463–1494)

CONSIDER

Consider when thou art movèd to be wroth,
  He who was God and of all men the best,
Seeing Himself scorned and scourgèd both,
  And as a thief between two thievès threst,
  With all rebuke and shame; yet from His breast
Came never sign of wrath or of disdain,
But patiently endurèd all the pain—

Think on the very lamentable pain,
  Think on the piteous cross of woeful Christ,
Think on His blood beat out at every vein,
Think on His precious heart carvèd in twain;
  Think how for thy redemption all was wrought,
  Let Him not lose what He so dear hath bought.

From the Italian, by Thomas More

Ludovico Ariosto
(1474–1533)

SONETTO

O benign Father, how can I believe Thou art
  In heaven and hearest my tepid pleas,
  When as I cry, undo my tongue!
  Thou see'st how much my heart enjoys the snare?

O knower of truth, unknot it for me,
  And gaze not on while my every sense denies it . . .

But afore I am condemned to Charon's ship
And dragged off to hell.

Excuse my error, eternal Lord, this wretched
Habit, by which, it seems, I cover mine eyes:
So little can I good from evil tell.

To pity a penitent soul is but a mortal's act;
But to drag him back from hell, against his will,
Is Thy power alone, Saving Lord.

From the Italian, by G.-Gabriel Gisondi

Michelangelo Buonarroti

(1475–1564)

NO MORTAL THING ENTHRALLED . . .

No mortal thing enthralled these longing eyes
When perfect peace in thy fair face I found;
But far within, where all is holy ground,
My soul felt Love, her comrade of the skies:
For she was born with God in Paradise;
Nor all the shows of beauty shed around
This fair false world her wings to earth have bound:
Unto the Love of Loves aloft she flies.
Nay, things that suffer death, quench not the fire
of deathless spirits; nor eternity
Serves sordid Time, that withers all things rare.
Not love but lawless impulse is desire:
That slays the soul; our love makes still more fair
Our friends on earth, fairer in death on high.

From the Italian, by John Addington Symonds

PERCHANCE THAT I MIGHT LEARN . . .

Perchance that I might learn what pity is,
    That I might laugh at erring men no more,
    Secure in my own strength as heretofore,
    My soul hath fallen from her state of bliss:
Nor know I under any flag but this
    How fighting I may 'scape those perils sore,
    Or how survive the rout and horrid roar
    Of adverse hosts, if I thy succor miss.
O flesh! O blood! O cross! O pain extreme!
    By you may those foul sins be purified,
    Wherein my fathers were, and I was born!
Lo, Thou alone art good: let Thy supreme
    Pity my state of evil cleanse and hide—
    So near to death, so far from God, forlorn.

From the Italian, by John Addington Symonds

NOW HATH MY LIFE . . .

Now hath my life across a stormy sea
    Like a frail bark reached that wide port where all
    Are bidden, ere the final reckoning fall
    Of good and evil for eternity.
Now know I well how that fond phantasy
    Which made my soul the worshiper and thrall
    Of earthly art, is vain; how criminal
    Is that which all men seek unwillingly.
Those amorous thoughts which were so lightly dressed,
    What are they when the double death is nigh?
    The one I know for sure, the other dread.
Painting nor sculpture now can lull to rest
    My soul that turns to His great love on high,
    Whose arms to clasp us on the cross were spread.

From the Italian, by John Addington Symonds

The prayers I make will then be sweet indeed,
If Thou the spirit give by which I pray:
My unassisted heart is barren clay,
Which of its native self can nothing feed:
Of good and pious works Thou art the seed,
Which quickens only where Thou say'st it may;
Unless Thou show to us Thine own true way,
No man can find it: Father! Thou must lead.
Do Thou, then, breathe those thoughts into my mind
By which such virtue may in me be bred
That in Thy holy footsteps I may tread;
That fetters of my tongue do Thou unbind,
That I may have the power to sing of Thee,
And sound Thy praises everlastingly.

From the Italian, by William Wordsworth

Martin Luther

(1483–1546)

EIN' FESTE BURG

Our God, a Tower of Strength is He,
A goodly wall and weapon;
From all our need He helps us free,
That now to us doth happen.
  The old evil foe
  Doth in earnest grow,
  In grim armor dight,
  Much guile and great might;
On earth there is none like him.

Of our own might we nothing can;
We soon are unprotected;

There fighteth for us the right Man,
Whom God himself elected.
    Who is He; ye exclaim?
    Christus is his name,
    Lord of Sabaoth,
    Very God in troth;
The field He holds forever.

This world may full of Devils be,
All ready to devour us;
Yet not so sore afraid are we,
They shall not overpower us.
    This World's Prince, howe'er
    Fierce he may appear,
    He can harm us not,
    He is doomed, God wot!
One little word can slay him!

The Word they shall perforce let stand
And little thanks they merit!
For He is with us in the land,
With gifts of his own Spirit!
    Though they take our life,
    Goods, honors, child and wife,
    Let these pass away,
    Little gain have they;
The Kingdom still remaineth!

From the German, by Henry W. Longfellow

Thomas Wyatt

(1503–1542)

PSALM 130: DE PROFUNDIS

From depth of sin and from a deep despair,
   From depth of death, from depth of heart's sorrow,
   From this deep cave of darkness deep repair,
Thee have I called, O Lord, to be my borrow;
   Thou in my voice, O Lord, perceive and hear
   My heart, my hope, my plaint, my overthrow,
My will to rise: and let by grant appear
   That to my voice Thine ears do well intend.
   No place so far that to Thee is not near;
No depth so deep that Thou ne mayst extend
   Thine ear thereto: hear then my woeful plaint.
   For, Lord, if Thou do observe what men offend
And put Thy native mercy in restraint,
   If just exaction demand recompense,
   Who may endure, O Lord? Who shall not faint
At such accompt? Dread, and not reverence
   Should so reign large. But Thou seeks rather love.
   For in Thy hand is mercy's residence,
By hope whereof Thou dost our hearts move.
   I in Thee, Lord, have set my confidence;
   My soul such trust doth evermore approve.
Thy holy word of eterne excellence,
   Thy mercy's promise that is alway just,
   Have been my stay, my pillar and pretense.
My soul in God hath more desirous trust
   Than hath the watchman looking for the day,
   By the relief to quench of sleep the thrust.
Let Israel trust unto the Lord alway,
   For grace and favor earn His property;
   Plenteous ransom shall come with Him, I say,
And shall redeem all our iniquity.

Attributed to Francis Xavier

(1506–1552)

O DEUS! EGO AMO TE'

Thou art my God, sole object of my love;
Not for the hope of endless joys above;
Not for the fear of endless pains below,
Which they who love thee not must undergo.

For me, and such as me, thou deign'st to bear
An ignominious cross, the nails, the spear:
A thorny crown transpierc'd thy sacred brow,
While bloody sweats from ev'ry member flow.

For me in tortures thou resign'd'st thy breath,
Embrac'd me on the cross, and sav'd me by thy death.
And can these suff'rings fail my heart to move?
What but thyself can now deserve my love?

Such as then was, and is, thy love to me,
Such is, and shall be still, my love to thee—
To thee, Redeemer! Mercy's sacred spring!
My God, my Father, Maker, and my King!

From the Latin, by Alexander Pope

John Calvin

(1509–1564)

SALUTATION À JÉSUS-CHRIST

I greet thee, who my sure Redeemer art,
My only trust and Saviour of my heart!
    Who so much toil and woe
    And pain didst undergo,
For my poor, worthless sake:
    We pray thee, from our hearts,
    All idle griefs and smarts
And foolish cares to take.

Thou are the true and perfect gentleness,
No harshness hast thou, and no bitterness:'
    Make us to taste and prove,
    Make us adore and love,
The sweet grace found in thee:
    With longing to abide
    Ever at thy side,
In thy sweet unity.

Poor banished exiles, wretched sons of Eve,
Full of all sorrows, unto thee we grieve;
    To thee we bring our sighs,
    Our groanings, and our cries:
Thy pity, Lord, we crave;
    We take the sinner's place,
    And pray thee, of thy grace,
To pardon and to save.

From the French, by Mrs. Smith

Teresa of Avila

(1515–1582)

IF, LORD, THY LOVE FOR ME IS STRONG

If, Lord, Thy love for me is strong
As this which binds me unto Thee,
What holds me from Thee, Lord, so long,
What holds Thee, Lord, so long from me?

O soul, what then desirest thou?
—Lord, I would see Thee, who thus choose Thee.
What fears can yet assail thee now?
—All that I fear is but to lose Thee.

Love's whole possession I entreat,
Lord, make my soul Thine own abode,
And I will build a nest so sweet
It may not be too poor for God.

O soul in God hidden from sin,
What more desires for thee remain,
Save but to love, and love again,
And, all on flame with love within,
Love on, and turn to love again?

From the Spanish, by Arthur Symons

LET MINE EYES SEE THEE

Let mine eyes see Thee,
Sweet Jesus of Nazareth,
Let mine eyes see Thee,
And then see death.

Let them see that care
Roses and jessamine;
Seeing Thy face most fair
All blossoms are therein.
Flower of seraphim,
Sweet Jesus of Nazareth,
Let mine eyes see Thee,
And then see death.

Nothing I require
Where my Jesus is;
Anguish all desire,
Saving only this;
All my help is His,
He only succoureth.
Let mine eyes see Thee,
Sweet Jesus of Nazareth,
Let mine eyes see Thee,
And then see death.

From the Spanish, by Arthur Symons

Joachim du Bellay

(1525–1560)

From THE VISIONS

It was the time, when rest, soft sliding down
   From heavens hight into men's heavy eyes,
In the forgetfulness of sleep doth drown
   The careful thoughts of mortal miseries;
Then did a ghost before mine eyes appear,
   On that great rivers bank, that runs by Rome;
Which, calling me by name, bade me to rear
   My looks to heaven, whence all good gifts do come,
And crying loud, "Lo! now behold," quote he,

"What under this great temple placed is:
Lo, all is nought but flying vanity!"
So I, that know this world's inconstancies,
Since only God surmounts all times decay,
In God alone my confidence do stay.

From the French, by Edmund Spenser

Luis de León

(1528–1591)

THE LIFE OF THE BLESSED

Region of life and light!
Land of the good whose earthly toils are o'er!
Nor frost nor heat may blight
Thy vernal beauty, fertile shore,
Yielding thy blessed fruits for evermore!

There, without crook or sling,
Walks the Good Shepherd; blossoms white and red
Round his meek temples cling;
And, to sweet pastures led,
His own loved flock beneath his eye is fed.

He guides, and near him they
Follow delighted; for he makes them go
Where dwells eternal May,
And heavenly roses blow,
Deathless, and gathered but again to grow.

He leads them to the height
Named of the infinite and long-sought Good,
And fountains of delight;
And where his feet have stood,
Springs up, along the way, their tender food.

And when, in the mid skies,
The climbing sun has reached his highest bound,

Reposing as he lies,
With all his flock around,
He witches the still air with numerous sound.

From his sweet lute flow forth
Immortal harmonies, of power to still
All passions born of earth,
And draw the ardent will
Its destiny of goodness to fulfill.

Might but a little part,
A wandering breath, of that high melody
Descend into my heart,
And change it till it be
Transformed and swallowed up, O love! in thee:

Ah! then my soul should know,
Beloved! where thou liest at noon of day;
And from this place of woe
Released, should take its way
To mingle with thy flock, and never stray.

From the Spanish, by William Cullen Bryant

Anonymous

(Sixteenth century)

I KNOW A ROSE-TREE SPRINGING

I know a rose-tree springing
    Forth from an ancient root,
As men of old were singing.
    From Jesse came the shoot
    That bore a blossom bright
Amid the cold of winter,
    When half-spent was the night.

This rose-tree, blossom-laden,
    Whereof Isaiah spake,

Is Mary, spotless maiden,
  Who mothered, for our sake,
  The little child, new-born
By God's eternal counsel
  On that first Christmas morn.

O flower, whose fragrance tender
  With sweetness fills the air,
Dispel in glorious splendor
  The darkness everywhere;
  True man, yet very God,
From sin and death now save us,
  And share our every load.

Anonymous translation from the German

Fernando de Herrera

(1534?–1597)

THE DISEMBODIED SPIRIT

Pure Spirit! that within a form of clay
Once veiled the brightness of thy native sky;
In dreamless slumber sealed thy burning eye,
Nor heavenward sought to wing thy flight away!
  He that chastised thee did at length unclose
Thy prison doors, and give thee sweet release,
Unloosed the mortal coil, eternal peace
Received thee to its stillness and repose.
  Look down once more from thy celestial dwelling,
Help me to rise and be immortal there—
An earthly vapor melting into air;—
  For my whole soul with secret ardor swelling,
From earth's dark mansion struggles to be free,
And longs to soar away and be at rest with thee.

From the Spanish, by Henry W. Longfellow

John of the Cross

(1542–1591)

ON A BLACK NIGHT

On a black night,
   burning with love's desire
   and excited by its danger
   I left my prison house,
   unseen, covered by the calm stillness
   of the night.

Darkness safely hiding me,
   I descended by a hidden stair—
   excited by love's danger.

Darkness covered my escape
   and the calm stillness of the night.

Dangerous night,
   secret night,
   no one could see me—
Blinded to everything,
   I saw only by the flame burning in my heart.

It guided me better than the light
   of the noonday sun—
   to Him, my love, awaiting me . . .

Oh night my guide,
   Oh night more beautiful than the day,
   Oh night that fused the two of us,
   lover and beloved!

On my breast,
   covered with flowers
   picked for Him alone,

He slept
   and I kissed him all over
   as the breezes hovered around us.

Breezes down the castle wall—
   my fingers through his hair,
   falling, gently, serenely.
His hand, wounding my neck,
   suspending all my senses.

I lay oblivious to myself
   with my face against His—
   everything ceased,
   my being fled
   to fade among the flowers.

From the Spanish, by Anthony S. Mercatante

OH, LIFE-GIVING FLAME OF LOVE

Oh, life-giving flame of love—
   tenderly wounding me to my inner being,
   I beg you, be bold,
   cut the cord that ties us in this sweet embrace!

You cauterize my wound
   and I burn with pleasure.
Your loving and delicate hands touch me
   and I taste eternity.
You dissolve my being
   yet you give me life.

A flame, clear and transparent
   burns deep inside me where once only shadows lived,
   giving me warmth and light,
   awaking all love in me.

How loving and soft are you
   lying upon my breasts—
   which are for you alone—

Your honeyed breath is filled with grace and glory.
Ah, how tenderly you make me love!

From the Spanish, by Anthony S. Mercatante

THE SOUL THAT LONGS FOR GOD

My life is not here—
 Not in myself,
 Not in my soul,
 Without God,
 God who is Life.

Can I wait for Life?
 Death, that is—
 Dying, that I do not die, to see God.
 This life that I live
  is without Life—
 Dying to see God.

Listen God, to what I say—
 I do not love this life.
 This life of dying because
  I do not die.

Without pain of death
My soul can live without life.
 Pity me, my soul,
 My soul that is saved from the death
  I am dying to die.

The fish that leaves the water
Can ease the pain of death—
 in death at last.
What can make death equal to Life?
 To my sad life,
 If I live more,
  Do I die more?

When I think that I can ease my pain
If I see Your Sacrifice,
It makes me sadder that I cannot touch you.
All because I long to see God and die,
  Dying so that I cannot die.

God, if it delights me,
Hoping to see you—then
Seeing that I can lose you
Increases my sorrow.
I am living in such dread—
  Hoping, waiting to die, destroys me.
  Dying so that I do not die.

Save me from that Death, God,
  Give me Life.
Don't hold me in those bonds,
  Those strong bonds.
Look how I long to see you.
My aching is as complete as my dying,
My dying so that my soul will not die.

I will cry for my dying now
And for my living as well
In such a sparing way as my sins are cried.
Oh, God, when will it be?
When can I say at last
That I live because I do not die?

From the Spanish, by John R. Matthews

SUM OF PERFECTION

Forgetting all created things,
Remembering the Creator.
Looking inwardly—
Loving the Lover.

From the Spanish, by Anthony S. Mercatante

Torquato Tasso

(1544–1595)

From JERUSALEM DELIVERED

The Christian army's great and puissant guide,
To assault the town that all his thoughts had bent,
Did ladders, rams, and engines huge provide,
When reverend Peter to him gravely went,
And drawing him with sober grace aside,
With words severe thus told his high intent;
    "Right well, my lord, these earthly strengths you move,
    But let us first begin from Heaven above:

"With public prayer, zeal and faith devout,
The aid, assistance, and the help obtain
Of all the blessèd of the heavenly rout,
With whose support you conquest sure may gain;
First let the priests before thine armies stout
With sacred hymns their holy voices strain.
    And thou and all thy lords and peers with thee,
    Of godliness and faith examples be."

Thus spake the hermit grave in words severe:
Godfrey allowed his counsel, sage, and wise,
"Of Christ the Lord," quoth he, "thou servant dear,
I yield to follow thy divine advice,
And while the princes I assemble here,
The great procession, songs and sacrifice,
    With Bishop William, thou and Ademare,
    With sacred and with solemn pomp prepare."

Next morn the bishops twain, the heremite,
And all the clerks and priests of less estate,
Did in the middest of the camp unite
Within a place for prayer consecrate,
Each priest adorned was in a surplice white,

The bishops donned their albes and copes of state,
   Above their rochets buttoned fair before,
   And mitres on their heads like crowns they wore.

Peter alone, before, spread to the wind
The glorious sign of our salvation great,
With easy pace the choir come all behind,
And hymns and psalms in order true repeat,
With sweet respondence in harmonious kind
Their humble song the yielding air doth beat,
   Lastly, together went the reverened pair
   Of prelates sage, William and Ademare.

The mighty duke came next, as princes do,
Without companion, marching all alone,
The lords and captains then came two and two,
The soldiers for their guard were armed each one;
With easy pace thus ordered, passing through
The trench and rampire, to the fields they gone,
   No thundering drum, no trumpet shrill they hear,
   Their godly music psalms and prayers were.

To thee, O Father, Son, and sacred Sprite,
One true, eternal, everlasting King;
To Christ's dear mother, Mary, virgin bright,
Psalms of thanksgiving and of praise they sing;
To them that angels down from heaven to fight
Gainst the blasphemous beast and dragon bring;
   To him also that our Saviour good,
   Washéd the sacred font in Jordan's flood.

. . . .

Singing and saying thus, the camp devout
Spread forth her zealous squadrons broad and wide;
Toward mount Olivet went all this route,
So called of olive trees the hills which hide,
A mountain known by fame the world throughout,
Which riseth on the city's eastern side,
   From it divided by the valley green
   Of Josaphat, that fills the space between.

Hither the armies went, and chanted shrill,
That all the deep and hollow dales resound;
From hollow mounts and caves in every hill,
A thousand echoes also sung around,
It seemed some choir, that sung with art and skill,
Dwelth in those savage dens and shady ground,
    For oft resounded from the banks they hear,
    The name of Christ and of his mother dear.

Upon the walls the Pagans old and young
Stood hushed and still, amated and amazed,
At their grave order and their humble song,
At their strange pomp and customs new they gazed:
But when the show they had beholden long,
An hideous yell the wicked miscreants raised,
    That with vile blasphemies the mountains hoar,
    The woods, the waters, and the valleys roar.

But yet the sacred notes the hosts proceed,
Though blasphemies they hear and cursèd things;
So with Apollo's harp Pan tunes his reed,
So adders hiss where Philomela sings;
Nor flying darts nor stones the Christians dreed,
Nor arrows shot, nor quarries cast from slings:
    But with assurèd faith, as dreading naught,
    The holy work begun to end they brought.

A table set they on the mountain's height
To minister theron the sacrament,
In golden candlesticks a hollowed light
At either end of virgin wax there brent;
In costly vestments sacred William dight,
With fear and trembling to the altar went,
    And prayer there and service loud begins,
    Both for his own and all the army's sins.

Humbly they heard his words that stood him nigh,
The rest far off upon him bent their eyes,
But when he ended had the service high,

"You servants of the Lord depart," he cries:
His hands he lifted then up to the sky,
And blessed all those warlike companies;
　　And they dismissed returned the way they came
　　Their order as before, their pomp the same.

From the Italian, by Edward Fairfax

Anonymous

(Ca. fifteenth century)

THE DREAM OF MARY

"Mother, mother, Mary, most holy,
　　where did you spend last night?"
"I spent last night in Jerusalem,
　　in God's church near His altar:
My sleep was restless and I dreamed,
　　a dream most strange, my son.
I gave birth to a son, Christ, the king,
　　and wrapped him in swaddling clothes."
Jesus, the Christ, said to holy Mary:
　　"O mother, mother! Do not tell me more.
I know what this dream means—
　　I will interpret it for you.
By the Jordan river grew a sacred tree,
　　a cypress, and it became the Cross,
Life-giving and wondrous Cross of Christ.
　　On that Cross I shall die . . ."

On Friday, before the Jewish Sabbath,
　　they came and crucified the Christ.
They nailed His hands and feet to the Cross.
　　His side was pierced with a spear,
His body beaten with a rod, His head bruised.
　　Mary heard of this and ran weeping to Him:
"My son, my son, why must you suffer so?

What shall now happen to your mother?"
"Do not cry, mother, Mary most holy,
  I will not leave you alone—
John, my beloved friend, will comfort you.
  Now I must die, mother dearest, but
On the third day I shall rise again:
  I will then come from heaven, mother,
With all its angels to bury your body.
  Your face I will paint on an icon,
Placing it in God's church near His altar.
  The faithful will pray to God,
See your holy icon, and give glory to me,
  the Christ, God the almighty."

Glory, glory, glory, to Christ, our God.

From the Russian, by Stephen Marks

William Baldwin

(Fl. 1547–1549)

CHRIST TO HIS SPOUSE

Lo, thou, my Love, art fair;
Myself have made thee so;
Yea, thou art fair indeed,
Wherefore thou shalt not need
In beauty to despair;
For I accept thee so,
    For fair.

For fair, because thine eyes
Are like the culvers' white,
Whose simpleness in deed
All others do exceed:
Thy judgement wholly lies
In true sense of sprite
    Most wise.

103

Edmund Spenser

(1552–1599)

AN HYMN
OF HEAVENLY LOVE

Love, lift me up upon thy golden wings
From this base world unto thy heaven's height,
Where I may see those admirable things
Which there thou workest by thy sovereign might,
Far above feeble reach of earthly sight,
That I thereof an heavenly hymn may sing
Unto the God of love, high heaven's king.

Many lewd lays—ah woe is me the more—
In praise of that mad fit which fools call love
I have in th' heat of youth made heretofore,
That in light wits did loose affection move;
But all those follies now I do reprove,
And turnèd have the tenor of my string,
The heavenly praises of true love to sing.

And ye that wont with greedy vain desire
To read my fault, and wondering at my flame
To warm yourselves at my wide sparkling fire,
Sith now that heat is quenchèd, quench my blame,
And in her ashes shroud my dying shame;
For who my passèd follies now pursues
Begins his own, and my old fault renews.

Before this world's great frame, in which all things
Are now contained, found any being-place,
Ere flitting Time could wag his eyas wings
About the mighty bound which doth embrace
The rolling spheres and parts their hours by space,
That high eternal power, which now doth move
In all these things, moved in itself by love.

It loved itself because itself was fair—
For fair is loved—and of itself begot
Like to itself, his eldest son and heir,
Eternal, pure, and void of sinful blot,
The firstling of his joy, in whom no jot
Of love's dislike or pride was to be found,
Whom he therefore with equal honor crowned.

With him he reigned, before all time prescribed,
In endless glory and immortal might,
Together with that third from them derived,
Most wise, most holy, most almighty sprite,
Whose kingdom's throne no thought of earthly wight
Can comprehend. Much less my trembling verse
With equal words can hope it to rehearse.

Yet O most blessed spirit, pure lamp of light,
Eternal spring of grace and wisdom true,
Vouchsafe to shed into my barren sprite
Some little drop of thy celestial dew,
That may my rhymes with sweet infuse imbrue;
And give me words equal unto my thought,
To tell the marvels by thy mercy wrought.

Yet being pregnant still with powerful grace,
And full of fruitful love, that loves to get
Things like himself, and to enlarge his race,
His second brood—though not in power so great,
Yet full of beauty—next he did beget,
An infinite increase of angels bright,
All glistering glorious in their maker's light.

To them the heavens' illimitable height—
Not this round heaven which we from hence behold—
Adorned with thousand lamps of burning light,
And with ten thousand gems of shining gold,
He gave as their inheritance to hold,
That they might serve him in eternal bliss,
And be partakers of those joys of his.

There they in their trinal triplicities
About him wait, and on his will depend,
Either with nimble wings to cut the skies,
When he them on his messages doth send,
Or on his own dread presence to attend,
Where they behold the glory of his light,
And carol hymns of love both day and night.

Both day and night is unto them all one,
For he his beams doth still to them extend,
That darkness there appeareth never none;
Ne hath their day, ne hath their bliss an end,
But there their termless time in pleasure spend.
Ne ever should their happiness decay,
Had not they dared their lord to disobey.

But pride impatient of long-resting peace,
Did puff them up with greedy bold ambition,
That they gan cast their state how to increase
Above the fortune of their first condition,
And sit in God's own seat without commission.
The brightest angel, even the child of light,
Drew millions more against their God to fight.

Th' Almighty seeing their so bold assay,
Kindled the flame of his consuming ire,
And with his only breath them blew away
From heaven's height, to which they did aspire,
To deepest hell, and lake of damnèd fire,
Where they in darkness and dread horror dwell,
Hating the happy light from which they fell.

So that next offspring of the Maker's love,
Next to himself in glorious degree,
Degendering to hate, fell from above
Through pride—for pride and love may ill agree—
And now of sin to all ensample be.
How then can sinful flesh itself assure,
Sith purest angels fell to be impure?

But that eternal fount of love and grace,
Still flowing forth his goodness unto all,
Now seeing left a waste and empty place
In his wide palace through those angels' fall,
Cast to supply the same, and to install
A new unknowen colony therein,
Whose root from earth's base groundwork should begin.

Therefore of clay—base, vile, and next to nought,
Yet formed by wondrous skill, and by his might,
According to an heavenly pattern wrought,
Which he had fashioned in his wise foresight—
He man did make, and breathed a living sprite
Into his face most beautiful and fair,
Endued with wisdom's riches, heavenly, rare.

Such he him made that he resemble might
Himself, as mortal thing immortal could;
Him to be lord of every living wight
He made by love out of his own like mold,
In whom he might his mighty self behold.
For love doth love the thing beloved to see,
That like itself in lovely shape may be.

But man, forgetful of his maker's grace
No less than angels whom he did ensue,
Fell from the hope of promised heavenly place
Into the mouth of death, to sinners due;
And all his offspring into thralldom threw,
Where they forever should in bonds remain
Of never dead, yet ever dying pain.

Till that great Lord of Love, which him at first
Made of mere love, and after likèd well,
Seeing him lie like creature long accursed
In that deep horror of despairèd hell,
Him wretch in dole would let no longer dwell,
But cast out of that bondage to redeem,
And pay the price, all were his debt extreme.

Out of the bosom of eternal bliss,
In which he reignèd with his glorious sire,
He down descended, like a most demiss
And abject thrall, in flesh's frail attire,
That he for him might pay sin's deadly hire,
And him restore unto that happy state
In which he stood before his hapless fate.

In flesh at first the guilt committed was;
Therefore in flesh it must be satisfied.
Nor spirit, nor angel, though they man surpass,
Could make amends to God for man's misguide,
But only man himself, who self did slide.
So taking flesh of sacred virgin's womb,
For man's dear sake he did a man become.

And that most blessed body, which was born
Without all blemish or reproachful blame,
He freely gave to be both rent and torn
Of cruel hands; who with despiteful shame
Reviling him, that them most vile became,
At length him nailèd on a gallow tree,
And slew the just by most unjust decree.

O huge and most unspeakable impression
Of love's deep wound, that pierced the piteous heart
Of that dear Lord with so entire affection,
And sharply launching every inner part,
Dolors of death into his soul did dart,
Doing him die that never it deserved,
To free his foes, that from his hest had swerved.

What heart can feel least touch of so sore launch,
Or thought can think the depth of so dear wound?
Whose bleeding source their streams yet never staunch,
But still do flow, and freshly still redound,
To heal the sores of sinful souls unsound,
And cleanse the guilt of that infected crime,
Which was enrooted in all fleshly slime.

O blessed well of love, O flower of grace,
O glorious morning star, O lamp of light,
Most lively image of thy Father's face,
Eternal King of Glory, Lord of Might,
Meek Lamb of God before all worlds behight—
How can we thee requite for all this good?
Or what can prize that thy most precious blood?

Yet nought thou askst in lieu of all this love
But love of us for guerdon of thy pain.
Ay me, what can us less than that behoove?
Had he requirèd life of us again,
Had it been wrong to ask his own with gain?
He gave us life, he it restorèd lost;
Then life were least, that us so little cost.

But he our life hath left unto us free,
Free that was thrall, and blessèd that was band;
Ne aught demands but that we loving be,
As he himself hath loved us aforehand,
And bound thereto with an eternal band
Him first to love that us so dearly bought,
And next, our brethren to his image wrought.

Him first to love, great right and reason is:
Who first to us our life and being gave;
And after, when we farèd had amiss,
Us wretches from the second death did save;
And last, the food of life, which now we have,
Even himself in his dear sacrament,
To feed our hungry souls unto us lent.

Then next to love our brethren, that were made
Of that self mold and that self maker's hand
That we, and to the same again shall fade
Where they shall have like heritage of land,
However here on higher steps we stand;
Which also were with self same price redeemed
That we, however of us light esteemed.

And were they not, yet since that loving Lord
Commanded us to love them for his sake—
Even for his sake, and for his sacred word,
Which in his last bequest he to us spake—
We should them love, and with their needs partake,
Knowing that whatso'er to them we give
We give to him, by whom we all do live.

Such mercy he by his most holy read
Unto us taught, and to approve it true
Ensampled it by his most righteous deed,
Showing us mercy—miserable crew—
That we the like should to the wretches shew,
And love our brethren, thereby to approve
How much himself, that lovèd us, we love.

Then rouse thyself, O earth, out of thy soil,
In which thou wallowest like to filthy swine,
And dost thy mind in dirty pleasures moil,
Unmindful of that dearest Lord of thine.
Lift up to him thy heavy clouded eyne,
That thou his sovereign bounty mayst behold,
And read through love his mercies manifold.

Begin from first, where he encradled was
In simple cratch, wrapped in a wad of hay,
Between the toilful ox and humble ass;
And in what rags, and in how base array,
The glory of our heavenly riches lay,
When him the silly shepherds came to see,
Whom greatest princes sought on lowest knee.

From thence, read on the story of his life:
His humble carriage, his unfaulty ways,
His cankered foes, his fights, his toil, his strife,
His pains, his poverty, his sharp assays,
Through which he passed his miserable days,
Offending none, and doing good to all,
Yet being maliced both of great and small.

And look at last how of most wretched wights
He taken was, betrayed, and false accused;
How with most scornful taunts and fell despites
He was reviled, disgraced, and foul abused;
How scourged, how crowned, how buffeted, how bruised;
And lastly how twixt robbers crucified,
With bitter wounds through hands, through feet and side.

Then let thy flinty heart that feels no pain
Empiercèd be with pitiful remorse;
And let thy bowels bleed in every vein
At sight of his most sacred heavenly corse,
So torn and mangled with malicious force;
And let thy soul, whose sins his sorrows wrought,
Melt into tears and groan in grievèd thought.

With sense whereof whilst so thy softened spirit
Is inly touched, and humbled with meek zeal,
Through meditation of his endless merit,
Lift up thy mind to th' author of thy weal,
And to his sovereign mercy do appeal;
Learn him to love that lovèd thee so dear,
And in thy breast his blessed image bear.

With all thy heart, with all thy soul and mind,
Thou must him love, and his behests embrace.
All other loves, with which the world doth blind
Weak fancies and stir up affections base,
Thou must renounce and utterly displace,
And give thyself unto him full and free,
That full and freely gave himself to thee.

Then shalt thou feel thy spirit so possessed
And ravished with devouring great desire
Of his dear self, that shall thy feeble breast
Inflame with love and set thee all on fire
With burning zeal through every part entire,
That in no earthly thing thou shalt delight,
But in his sweet and amiable sight.

Thenceforth all world's desire will in thee die,
And all earth's glory on which men do gaze
Seem dirt and dross in thy pure-sighted eye,
Compared to that celestial beauty's blaze,
Whose glorious beams all fleshly sense doth daze
With admiration of their passing light,
Blinding the eyes and lumining the sprite.

Then shall thy ravished soul inspirèd be
With heavenly thoughts, far above human skill,
And thy bright radiant eyes shall plainly see
Th' idea of his pure glory present still
Before thy face, that all thy spirits shall fill
With sweet enragement of celestial love,
Kindled through sight of those fair things above.

Walter Raleigh

(1552–1618)

THE PASSIONATE MAN'S PILGRIMAGE

Give me my scallop-shell of quiet,
My staff of faith to walk upon,
My scrip of joy, immortal diet,
My bottle of salvation,
My gown of glory, hope's true gage,
And thus I'll take my pilgrimage.

Blood must be my body's balmer,
No other balm will there be given,
Whilst my soul like a white palmer
Travels to the land of heaven,
Over the silver mountains,
Where spring the nectar fountains;
And there I'll kiss
The bowl of bliss,
And drink my eternal fill

On every milken hill.
My soul will be a-dry before,
But after it will ne'er thirst more.

And by the happy blissful way
More peaceful pilgrims I shall see,
That have shook off their gowns of clay
And go appareled fresh like me.
I'll bring them first
To slake their thirst,
And then to taste those nectar suckets,
At the clear wells
Where sweetness dwells,
Drawn up by saints in crystal buckets.

And when our bottles and all we
Are filled with immortality,
Then the holy paths we'll travel,
Strewed with rubies thick as gravel,
Ceilings of diamonds, sapphire floors,
High walls of coral, and pearl bowers.

From thence tc heaven's bribeless hall
Where no corrupted voices brawl,
No conscience molten into gold,
Nor forged accusers bought and sold,
No cause deferred, nor vain-spent journey,
For there Christ is the king's attorney,
Who pleads for all without degrees,
And he hath angels, but no fees.

When the grand twelve million jury
Of our sins and sinful fury,
'Gainst our souls black verdicts give,
Christ pleads his death, and then we live.
Be thou my speaker, taintless pleader,
Unblotted lawyer, true proceeder,
Thou movest salvation even for alms,
Not with a bribed lawyer's palms.

113

And this is my eternal plea
To Him that made heaven, earth, and sea,
Seeing my flesh must die so soon,
And want a head to dine next noon,
Just at the stroke when my veins start and spread,
Set on my soul an everlasting head.
Then am I ready, like a palmer fit,
To tread those blest paths which before I writ.

Philip Sidney

(1554–1586)

SINCE NATURE'S WORKS BE GOOD . . .

Since Nature's works be good, and death doth serve
As Nature's work, why should we fear to die?
Since fear is vain but when it may preserve,
Why should we fear that which we cannot fly?
Fear is more pain than is the pain it fears,
Disarming human minds of native might;
While each conceit an ugly figure bears,
Which were not evil, well view'd in reason's light
Our only eyes, which dimm'd with passions be,
And scarce discern the dawn of coming day,
Let them be clear'd, and now begin to see
Our life is but a step in dusty way:
Then let us hold the bliss of peaceful mind,
Since this we feel, great loss we cannot find.

Fulke Greville

(1554–1628)

From CAELICA

Wrapped up, O Lord, in man's degeneration,
The glories of Thy truth, Thy joys eternal,
Reflect upon my soul's dark desolation,
And ugly prospects o'er the sprites infernal.
   Lord, I have sinned, and mine iniquity
   Deserves this hell; yet, Lord, deliver me.

Thy power and mercy never comprehended
Rest lively imaged in my conscience wounded;
Mercy to grace, and power to fear extended,
Both infinite, and I in both confounded.
   Lord, I have sinned, and mine iniquity
   Deserves this hell; yet, Lord, deliver me.

If from this depth of sin, this hellish grave,
And fatal absence from my Saviour's glory
I could implore His mercy, who can save,
And for my sins, not pains of sin, be sorry;
   Lord, from this horror of iniquity
   And hellish grave, Thou wouldst deliver me.

François de Malherbe

(1555–1628)

PARAPHRASE OF PSALM CXLV

At length, my soul! thy fruitless hopes give o'er,
Believe, believe the treach'rous world no more.
Shallow, yet swift, the stream of fortune flows,

Which some rude mind will always discompose;
As children birds, so men their bliss pursue,
Still out of reach, tho' ever in their view.

In vain, for all that empty greatness brings,
We lose our lives amidst the courts of kings,
And suffer scorn, and bend the supple knee;
The monarch dies—one moment's turn destroys
Long future prospects, and short present joys:
Oh unperforming, false mortality!

All is but dust, when once their breath is fled;
The fierce, the pompous majesty lies dead!
The world no longer trembles at their pow'r!
Ev'n in those tombs where their proud names survive,
Where still in breathing brass they seem to live,
Th' impartial worms that very dust devour.
The lofty styles of happy, glorious great,
The Lords of fortune, Arbiters of fate,
And Gods of war, lie lost within the grave!
Their mighty minions then come tumbling down,
They lose their flatt'rers as they lose their crown,
Forgot of ev'ry friend, and ev'ry slave!

From the French, by Alexander Pope

Lope de Vega

(1562–1635)

THE GOOD SHEPHERD: A SONNET

Shepherd! who with thine amorous, sylvan song
Hast broken the slumber that encompassed me,
Who mad'st Thy crook from the accursèd tree
On which Thy powerful arms were stretched so long!
    Lead me to mercy's ever-flowing fountains;
For Thou my shepherd, guard, and guide shalt be;
I will obey Thy voice, and wait to see

Thy feet all beautiful upon the mountains.
Hear, Shepherd, Thou who for Thy flock art dying,
Oh, wash away these scarlet sins, for Thou
Rejoicest at the contrite sinner's vow!
Oh, wait! to Thee my weary soul is crying,
Wait for me: Yet why ask it, when I see,
With feet nailed to the cross, Thou'rt waiting still for me!

From the Spanish, by Henry W. Longfellow

part four

Baroque Christian Poems

"Batter my heart, three-personed God. . . ."

The griffin, a mythical beast, half-eagle, half-lion, represents the dual nature of Christ—the human and divine. It serves as a symbol in the closing cantos of Dante's *Purgatorio*.

Robert Southwell

(1561?–1595)

THE BURNING BABE

As I in hoary winter's night stood shivering in the snow,
Surprised I was with sudden heat, which made my heart to glow;
And lifting up a fearful eye to view what fire was near,
A pretty Babe all burning bright, did in the air appear,
Who scorchèd with excessive heat, such floods of tears did shed,
As though His floods should quench His flames which with His tears
      were fed;
Alas! quoth He, but newly born, in fiery heats I fry,
Yet none approach to warm their hearts or feel my fire but I!
My faultless breast the furnace is, the fuel wounding thorns,
Love is the fire, and sighs the smoke, the ashes shame and scorns;
The fuel Justice layeth on, and Mercy blows the coals,
The metal in this furnace wrought are men's defiled souls,
For which, as now on fire I am to work them to their good,
So will I melt into a bath to wash them in My blood:
With this He vanished out of sight, and swiftly shrunk away,
And straight I callèd unto mind that it was Christmas-day.

Luis de Góngora

(1561–1627)

THE NATIVITY OF CHRIST

Today from the Aurora's bosom
A pink has fallen—a crimson blossom;
And oh, how glorious rests the hay
On which the fallen blossom lay!

When silence gently had unfurled
Her mantle over all below,
And crowned with winter's frost and snow,
Night swayed the sceptre of the world,
Amid the gloom descending slow
  Upon the monarch's frozen bosom
  A pink has fallen,—a crimson blossom.

The only flower the Virgin bore
(Aurora fair) within her breast,
She gave to earth, yet still possessed
Her virgin blossom as before;
That hay that colored drop caressed,—
  Received upon its faithful bosom
  That single flower,—a crimson blossom.

The manger, unto which 'twas given,
Even amid wintry snows and cold,
Within its fostering arms to fold
The blushing flower that fell from heaven,
Was as a canopy of gold.—
  A downy couch,—where on its bosom
  That flower had fallen,—that crimson blossom.

From the Spanish, by Henry W. Longfellow

Bartolomé Leonardo de Argensola

(1564–1631)

TO MARY MAGDALEN

Blessèd, yet sinful one, and broken-hearted!
The crowd are pointing at the thing forlorn,
In wonder and in scorn!
Thou weepest days of innocence departed;
Thou weepest, and thy tears have power to move
The Lord to pity and love.

The greatest of thy follies is forgiven,
Even for the least of all the tears that shine
On that pale cheek of thine.
Thou didst kneel down to Him who came from heaven,
Evil and ignorant, and thou shalt rise
Holy and pure and wise.

It is not much that to the fragrant blossom
The ragged briar should change, the bitter fir
Distil Arabian myrrh;
Nor that, upon the wintry desert's bosom,
The harvest should rise plenteous, and the swain
Bear home the abundant grain.

But come and see the bleak and barren mountains
Thick to their tops with roses; come and see
Leaves on the dry dead tree;
The perished plant, set out by living fountains,
Grow fruitful, and its beauteous branches rise,
Forever, to the skies!

From the Spanish, by William Cullen Bryant

John Donne

(1573–1631)

I AM A LITTLE WORLD MADE CUNNINGLY

I am a little world made cunningly
Of elements, and an angelic sprite,
But black sin hath betrayed to endless night
My world's both parts, and oh, both parts must die.
You which beyond that heaven which was most high
Have found new spheres, and of new lands can write,
Pour new seas in mine eyes, that so I might
Drown my world with my weeping earnestly,
Or wash it if it must be drowned no more;
But oh it must be burnt! Alas, the fire
Of lust and envy have burnt it heretofore,
And made it fouler; let their flames retire,
And burn me, O Lord, with a fiery zeal
Of Thee and Thy house, which doth in eating heal.

AS DUE BY MANY TITLES I RESIGN

As due by many titles I resign
Myself to thee, O God, first I was made
By thee, and for thee, and when I was decayed
Thy blood bought that, the which before was thine;
I am thy son, made with thyself to shine,
Thy servant, whose pains thou hast still repaid,
Thy sheep, thine image, and, till I betrayed
Myself, a temple of thy Spirit divine;
Why doth the devil then usurp on me?
Why doth he steal, nay ravish that's thy right?
Except thou rise and for thine own work fight,
Oh I shall soon despair, when I do see

That thou lov'st mankind well, yet wilt not choose me,
And Satan hates me, yet is loth to lose me.

AT THE ROUND EARTH'S IMAGINED CORNERS

At the round earth's imagined corners, blow
Your trumpets, angels, and arise, arise
From death, you numberless infinities
Of souls, and to your scattered bodies go;
All whom the flood did, and fire shall o'erthrow,
All whom war, dearth, age, agues, tyrannies,
Despair, law, chance, hath slain, and you whose eyes
Shall behold God, and never taste death's woe.
But let them sleep, Lord, and me mourn a space,
For if, above all these, my sins abound,
'Tis late to ask abundance of Thy grace
When we are there; here on this lowly ground,
Teach me how to repent; for that's as good
As if Thou hadst sealed my pardon with Thy blood.

BATTER MY HEART, THREE-PERSONED GOD

Batter my heart, three-personed God, for you
As yet but knock, breathe, shine, and seek to mend;
That I may rise and stand, o'erthrow me, and bend
Your force to break, blow, burn and make me new.
I, like an usurped town, to another due,
Labour to admit you, but oh, to no end;
Reason your viceroy in me, me should defend,
But is captived, and proves weak or untrue.
Yet dearly I love you, and would be loved fain,
But am betrothed unto your enemy:
Divorce me, untie, or break that knot again,
Take me to you, imprison me, for I
Except you enthrall me, never shall be free,
Nor ever chaste, except you ravish me.

125

IF POISONOUS MINERALS

If poisonous minerals, and if that tree
Whose fruit threw death on else immortal us,
If lecherous goats, if serpents envious
Cannot be damned, alas, why should I be?
Why should intent or reason, born in me,
Make sins, else equal, in me more heinous?
And mercy being easy and glorious
To God, in his stern wrath why threatens He?
But who am I that dare dispute with Thee,
O God? O, of thine only worthy blood
And my tears make a heavenly Lethean flood,
And drown in it my sins' black memory.
That thou remember them, some claim as debt;
I think it mercy if thou wilt forget.

A HYMN TO CHRIST, AT THE AUTHOR'S LAST
GOING INTO GERMANY

In what torn ship soever I embark,
That ship shall be my emblem of Thy ark;
What sea soever swallow me, that flood
Shall be to me an emblem of Thy blood;
Though Thou with clouds of anger do disguise
Thy face, yet through that mask I know those eyes,
  Which, though they turn away sometimes,
    They never will despise.

I sacrifice this island unto Thee,
And all whom I loved there, and who love me;
When I have put our seas twixt them and me,
Put Thou Thy seas betwixt my sins and Thee.
As the tree's sap doth seek the root below
In winter, in my winter now I go

126

Where none but Thee, th' eternal root
    Of true love, I may know.

Nor Thou nor Thy religion dost control
The amorousness of an harmonious soul
But Thou would'st have that love Thyself; as Thou
Art jealous, Lord, so I am jealous now;
Thou lov'st not, till from loving more, Thou free
My soul; whoever gives, takes liberty;
    Oh, if Thou car'st not whom I love,
      Alas, Thou lov'st not me.

Seal then this bill of my divorce to all
On whom those fainter beams of love did fall;
Marry those loves, which in youth scattered be
On fame, wit, hopes (false mistresses), to Thee.
Churches are best for prayer that have least light:
To see God only, I go out of sight;
    And to 'scape stormy days, I choose
      An everlasting night.

HYMN TO GOD MY GOD, IN MY SICKNESS

Since I am coming to that holy room
    Where, with Thy choir of saints for evermore,
I shall be made Thy music; as I come
    I tune the instrument here at the door,
    And what I must do then, think here before.

Whilst my physicians by their love are grown
    Cosmographers, and I their map, who lie
Flat on this bed, that by them may be shown
    That this is my southwest discovery
    Per fretum febris, by these straits to die.

I joy, that in these straits, I see my West;
    For, though their currents yield return to none,
What shall my West hurt me? As West and East

In all flat maps (and I am one) are one,
So death doth touch the resurrection.

Is the Pacific Sea my home? Or are
    The Eastern riches? Is Jerusalem?
Anyan, and Magellan, and Gibraltar,
    All straits, and none but straits, are ways to them,
    Whether where Japhet dwelt, or Cham, or Shem.

We think that Paradise and Calvary,
    Christ's cross, and Adam's tree, stood in one place;
Look, Lord, and find both Adams met in me;
    As the first Adam's sweat surrounds my face,
    May the last Adam's blood my soul embrace.

So, in his purple wrapped, receive me, Lord;
    By these his thorns give me his other crown;
And, as to others' souls I preached Thy word,
    Be this my text, my sermon to mine own;
    Therefore that he may raise the Lord throws down.

A HYMN TO GOD THE FATHER

Wilt thou forgive that sin where I begun,
    Which is my sin, though it were done before?
Wilt thou forgive that sin through which I run,
    And do run still, though still I do deplore?
When thou hast done, thou hast not done;
        For I have more.

Wilt thou forgive that sin which I have won
    Others to sin, and made my sin their door?
Wilt thou forgive that sin which I did shun
    A year or two, but wallowed in a score?
When thou hast done, thou hast not done;
        For I have more.

I have a sin of fear, that when I've spun
    My last thread, I shall perish on the shore;

128

Swear by thyself that at my death thy Son
  Shall shine as he shines now and heretofore;
And having done that, thou hast done;
    I fear no more.

Ben Jonson

(1572–1637)

A HYMN TO GOD THE FATHER

Hear me, O God!
  A broken heart
  Is my best part:
Use still thy rod
  That I may prove
  Therein, thy Love.

If thou hadst not
  Been stern to me,
  But left me free,
I had forgot
  Myself and thee.

For sin's so sweet,
  As minds ill bent
  Rarely repent,
Until they meet
  Their punishment.

Who more can crave
  Than thou hast done:
  That gav'st a Son
To free a slave?
  First made of nought;
  With All since bought.

Sin, Death, and Hell,
  His glorious Name

Quite overcame,
Yet I rebel
And slight the same.

But, I'll come in,
Before my loss
Me farther toss,
As sure to win,
Under his Cross.

Joost Van Den Vondel

(1587–1679)

THE HYMN OF ADAM

O Father, we approach Thy throne,
Who bidst the glorious sun arise,
All-good, almighty and all-wise
Great Source of all things, God alone!

We see Thee, brighter than the rays
Of the bright sun, we see Thee shine!
As in a fountain, light divine,
We see Thee, endless fount of days!

We see Thee who our frame hast wrought
With one swift word from senseless clay;
Waked with one glance of heavenly ray
Our never dying souls from naught.

Those souls Thou lightedst with the spark
At Thy pure fire; and gracious still,
Gav'st immortality, free-will,
And language not involved in dark!

From the Dutch, by John Bowring

Giles Fletcher, the Younger

(1588?–1638)

From CHRIST'S VICTORY AND TRIUMPH

Say, earth, why hast thou got thee new attire,
And stick'st thy habit full of daisies red?
Seems that thou dost to some high thought aspire,
And some new-found-out bridegroom mean'st to wed:
Tell me, ye trees, so fresh apparellèd,—
   So never let the spiteful canker waste you,
   So never let the heavens with lightning blast you,—
Why go you now so trimly dressed, or whither haste you?

Answer me, Jordan, why thy crooked tide
So often wanders from his nearest way,
As though some other way thy stream would slide,
And fain salute the place where something lay.
And you, sweet birds, that, shaded from the ray,
   Sit carolling and piping grief away,
   The while the lambs, to hear you, dance and play,
Tell me, sweet birds, what is it you so fain would say?

And thou, fair spouse of earth, that every year
Gett'st such a numerous issue of thy bride,
How chance thou hotter shin'st, and draw'st more near?
Sure thou somewhere some worthy sight hast spied,
That in one place for joy thou canst not bide:
   And you, dead swallows, that so lively now
   Through the flit air your wingèd passage row,
How could new life into your frozen ashes, flow?

Ye primroses and purple violets,
Tell me, why blaze ye from your leavy bed,
And woo men's hands to rent you from your sets,
As though you would somewhere be carrièd,

131

With fresh perfumes, and velvets garnishëd?
    But ah! I need not ask, 'tis surely so,
    You all would to your Savior's triumphs go,
There would ye all await, and humble homage do.

Robert Herrick

(1591–1674)

TO KEEP A TRUE LENT

Is this a fast, to keep
                    The larder lean,
                            And clean
From fat of veals and sheep?

Is it to quit the dish
                    Of flesh, yet still
                            To fill
The platter high with fish?

Is it to fast an hour
                    Or ragg'd to go,
                            Or show
A downcast look, and sour?

No; 'tis a fast to dole
                    Thy sheaf of wheat
                    And meat
Unto the hungry soul.

It is to fast from strife,
                    From old debate
                            And hate;
To circumcise thy life;

To show a heart grief-rent;
                            To starve thy sin,
                                Not bin.
And that's to keep thy Lent.

George Herbert

(1593–1632)

THE PULLEY

When God at first made man,
Having a glass of blessings standing by—
"Let us," said he, "pour on him all we can;
Let the world's riches, which dispersed lie,
　Contract into a span."

So strength first made a way,
Then beauty flowed, then wisdom, honor, pleasure:
When almost all was out, God made a stay,
Perceiving that, alone of all his treasure,
　Rest in the bottom lay.

"For if I should," said he,
"Bestow this jewel also on my creature,
He would adore my gifts instead of me,
And rest in nature, not the God of nature:
　So both should losers be.

"Yet let him keep the rest,
But keep them with repining restlessness;
Let him be rich and weary, that at least,
If goodness lead him not, yet weariness
　May toss him to my breast."

DISCIPLINE

Throw away Thy rod,
Throw away Thy wrath;
　O my God,
Take the gentle path.

For my heart's desire
Unto Thine is bent;

I aspire
To a full consent.

Not a word or look
I affect to own,
    But by book,
And Thy Book alone.

Though I fail, I weep;
Though I halt in pace,
    Yet I creep
To the throne of grace.

Then let wrath remove;
Love will do the deed;
    For with love
Stony hearts will bleed.

Love is swift of foot;
Love's a man of war,
    And can shoot,
And can hit from far.

Who can 'scape his bow?
That which wrought on Thee,
    Brought Thee low,
Needs must work on me.

Throw away Thy rod:
Though man frailties hath,
    Thou art God;
Throw away Thy wrath.

LOVE

Love bade me welcome; yet my soul drew back,
    Guilty of dust and sin.
But quick-eyed Love, observing me grow slack
    From my first entrance in,

Drew nearer to me, sweetly questioning
  If I lacked anything.

"A guest," I answered, "worthy to be here."
  Love said, "You shall be he."
"I, the unkind, ungrateful? Ah, my dear,
  I cannot look on Thee."
Love took my hand, and smiling, did reply,
  "Who made the eyes but I?"

"Truth, Lord, but I have marred them: let my shame
  Go where it doth deserve."
"And know you not," says Love, "who bore the blame?"
  "My dear, then I will serve."
"You must sit down," says Love, "and taste my meat."
  So I did sit and eat.

PRAYER

Prayer the Churches banquet, Angels age,
    God's breath in man returning to his birth,
    The soul in paraphrase, heart in pilgrimage,
The Christian plummet sounding heav'n and earth:

Engine against th'Almighty, sinners tower,
    Reversed thunder, Christ-side-piercing spear,
    The six-days—world transposing in an hour,
A kind of tune, which all things hear and fear;

Softness, and peace, and joy, and love, and bliss,
    Exalted Manna, gladness of the best,
    Heaven in ordinary, man well drest,
The milky way, the bird of Paradise,
    Church-bells beyond the stars heard, the souls blood,
    The land of spices; something understood.

Calderón de la Barca

(1600–1681)

THE HOLY EUCHARIST

Honey in the lion's mouth,
Emblem mystical, divine,
How the sweet and strong combine;
Cloven rock for Israel's drouth;
Treasure-house of golden grain
By our Joseph laid in store,
In his brethren's famine sore
Freely to dispense again;
Dew on Gideon's snowy fleece;
Well from bitter turned to sweet;
Shew-bread laid in order sweet,
Bread whose cost doth ne'er increase,
Though no rain in April fall;
Horeb's manna freely given
Showered in white dew from heaven,
Marvellous, angelical;
Weightiest bunch of Canaan's vine;
Cake to strengthen and sustain
Through long days of desert pain;
Salem's monarch's bread and wine;—
Thou the antidote shall be
Of my sickness and my sin,
Consolation, medicine,
Life and Sacrament to me.

From the Spanish, by Richard C. Trench

Violante do Ceo

(1601–1693)

THE NIGHT OF MARVELS

In such a marvellous night, so fair
   And full of wonder strange and new,
Ye shepherds of the vale, declare
   Who saw the greatest wonder? Who?

I saw the trembling fire look wan.
   I saw the sun shed tears of blood.
I saw a God become a man.
   I saw a man become a God.

O wondrous marvels! at the thought,
   The bosom's awe and reverence move,
But who such prodigies has wrought?
   What gave such wonders birth? 'Twas love!

What called from heaven that flame divine,
   Which streams in glory from above;
And bade it o'er earth's bosom shine,
   And bless us with its brightness? Love!

Who bade the glorious sun arrest
   His course, and o'er heaven's concave move
In tears,—the saddest, loneliest
   Of the celestial orbs? 'Twas love!

Who raised the human race so high,
   Even to the starry seats above,
That for our mortal progeny,
   A man became a God? 'Twas love!

Who humbled from the seats of light
   Their Lord, all human woes to prove;

137

Led the great source of day—to night;
  And made of God a man? 'Twas love!

Yes, love has wrought, and love alone,
  The victories all,—beneath,—above,—
And earth and heaven shall shout as one,
  The all-triumphant song of love.

The song through all heaven's arches ran,
  And told the wondrous tales aloud,—
The trembling fire that looked so wan,
  The weeping sun behind the cloud.
A God—a God! becomes a man!
  A mortal man becomes a God!

From the Portuguese, by John Bowring

Paul Gerhardt

(1607–1676)

ALL MY HEART THIS NIGHT REJOICES

All my heart this night rejoices,
As I hear,
Far and near,
Sweetest angel voices:
"Christ is born" their choirs singing,
Till the air,
Everywhere,
Now with joy is ringing.

Hark! a voice from yonder manger,
Soft and sweet,
Doth entreat,
"Flee from woe and danger;
Breathren, come from all that grieves you

You are free;
All you need
I will surely give you."

Come, then, let us hasten yonder;
Here let all,
Great and small,
Kneel in awe and wonder,
Love Him who with love is yearning;
Hail the Star
That from far
Bright with hope is burning.

Thee, dear Lord with heed I'll cherish,
Live to Thee,
And with Thee
Dying, shall not perish,
But shall dwell with Thee forever
Far on high
In the joy
That can alter never.

From the German, by Catherine Winkworth

John Milton

(1608–1674)

ON THE MORNING OF CHRIST'S NATIVITY

This is the month, and this the happy morn,
Wherein the Son of Heaven's eternal King,
Of wedded Maid and Virgin Mother born,
Our great redemption from above did bring;
For so the holy sages once did sing,
    That he our deadly forfeit should release,
And with his Father work us a perpetual peace.

That glorious form, that light unsufferable,
And that far-beaming blaze of majesty,
Wherewith he wont at Heaven's high council-table
To sit the midst of Trinal Unity,
He laid aside, and, here with us to be,
  Forsook the courts of everlasting day,
And chose with us a darksome house of mortal clay.

Say, Heavenly Muse, shall not thy sacred vein
Afford a present to the Infant God?
Hast thou no verse, no hymn, or solemn strain,
To welcome him to this his new abode,
Now while the heaven, by the sun's team untrod,
  Hath took no print of the approaching light,
And all the spangled host keep watch in squadrons bright?

See how from far upon the eastern road
The star-led wizards haste with odors sweet!
Oh! run; prevent them with thy humble ode,
And lay it lowly at his blessèd feet;
Have thou the honor first thy Lord to greet,
  And join thy voice unto the angel choir,
From out his secret altar touched with hallowed fire.

THE HYMN

It was the winter wild,
While the Heaven-born child
  All meanly wrapped in the rude manger lies;
Nature in awe to him
Had doffed her gaudy trim,
  With her great Master so to sympathize:
It was no season then for her
To wanton with the sun her lusty paramour.

Only with speeches fair
She woos the gentle air
  To hide her guilty front with innocent snow,
And on her naked shame,
Pollute with sinful blame,

140

The saintly veil of maiden white to throw,
Confounded, that her Maker's eyes
Should look so near upon her foul deformities.

But he, her fears to cease,
Sent down the meek-eyed Peace;
    She crowned with olive green came softly sliding
Down through the turning sphere,
His ready harbinger,
    With turtle wing the amorous clouds dividing,
And waving wide her myrtle wand,
She strikes a universal peace through sea and land.

No war, or battle's sound,
Was heard the world around;
    The idle spear and shield were high uphung;
The hookèd chariot stood,
Unstained with hostile blood;
    The trumpet spake not to the armèd throng;
And kings sate still with awful eye,
As if they surely knew their sovran Lord was by.

But peaceful was the night
Wherein the Prince of Light
    His reign of peace upon the earth began.
The winds, with wonder whist,
Smoothly the waters kissed,
    Whispering new joys to the mild oceàn,
Who now hath quite forgot to rave,
While birds of calm sit brooding on the charmèd wave.

The stars, with deep amaze,
Stand fixed in steadfast gaze,
    Bending one way their precious influence,
And will not take their flight,
For all the morning light,
    Or Lucifer that often warned them thence;
But in their glimmering orbs did glow,
Until their Lord himself bespake, and bid them go.

And, though the shady gloom
Had given day her room,
   The sun himself withheld his wonted speed,
And hid his head for shame,
As his inferior flame
   The new-enlightened world no more should need:
He saw a greater Sun appear
Than his bright throne or burning axletree could bear.

The shepherds on the lawn,
Or ere the point of dawn,
   Sat simply chatting in a rustic row;
Full little thought they than
That the mighty Pan
   Was kindly come to live with them below;
Perhaps their loves, or else their sheep,
Was all that did their silly thoughts so busy keep.

When such music sweet
Their hearts and ears did greet,
   As never was by mortal finger strook,
Divinely warbled voice
Answering the stringèd noise,
   As all their souls in blissful rapture took:
The air such pleasure loth to lose,
With thousand echoes still prolongs each heavenly close.

Nature that heard such sound
Beneath the hollow round
   Of Cynthia's seat, the airy region thrilling,
Now was almost won
To think her part was done,
   And that her reign had here its last fulfilling;
She knew such harmony alone
Could hold all Heaven and Earth in happier union.

At last surrounds their sight
A globe of circular light,
   That with long beams the shame-faced night arrayed,

The helmèd cherubim
And swordèd seraphim
    Are seen in glittering ranks with wings displayed,
Harping in loud and solemn quire,
With unexpressive notes to Heaven's new-born Heir.

Such music (as 'tis said)
Before was never made,
    But when of old the Sons of Morning sung,
While the Creator great
His constellations set,
    And the well-balanced world on hinges hung,
And cast the dark foundations deep,
And bid the weltering waves their oozy channel keep.

Ring out, ye crystal spheres!
Once bless our human ears,
    If ye have power to touch our senses so;
And let your silver chime
Move in melodious time;
    And let the bass of heaven's deep organ blow;
And with your ninefold harmony
Make up full consort to the angelic symphony.

For, if such holy song
Enwrap our fancy long,
    Time will run back and fetch the Age of Gold;
And speckled Vanity
Will sicken soon and die;
    And leprous Sin will melt from earthly mold;
And Hell itself will pass away,
And leave her dolorous mansions to the peering day.

Yea, Truth and Justice then
Will down return to men,
    Orbed in a rainbow; and, like glories wearing,
Mercy will sit between,
Throned in celestial sheen,
    With radiant feet the tissued clouds down steering;

And Heaven, as at some festival,
Will open wide the gates of her high palace-hall.

But wisest Fate says No,
This must not yet be so,
    The Babe lies yet in smiling infancy,
That on the bitter cross
Must redeem our loss,
    So both himself and us to glorify:
Yet first to those ychained in sleep,
The wakeful trump of doom must thunder through the deep,

With such a horrid clang
As on Mount Sinai rang,
    While the red fire and smold'ring clouds outbrake:
The agèd Earth aghast
With terror of that blast
    Shall from the surface to the center shake;
When at the world's last sessiòn,
The dreadful Judge in middle air shall spread his throne.

And then at last our bliss
Full and perfect is,
    But now begins; for from this happy day
The old Dragon under ground
In straiter limits bound,
    Not half so far casts his usurpèd sway,
And, wroth to see his kingdom fail,
Swinges the scaly horror of his folded tail.

The oracles are dumb,
No voice or hideous hum
    Runs through the archèd roof in words deceiving.
Apollo from his shrine
Can no more divine,
    With hollow shriek the steep of Delphos leaving.
No nightly trance or breathèd spell
Inspires the pale-eyed priest from the prophetic cell.

The lonely mountains o'er,
And the resounding shore,
    A voice of weeping heard, and loud lament;
From haunted spring and dale,
Edged with poplar pale,
    The parting Genius is with sighing sent,
With flower-inwoven tresses torn
The Nymphs in twilight shade of tangled thickets mourn.

In consecrated earth,
And on the holy hearth,
    The Lars and Lemures moan with midnight plaint;
In urns and altars round,
A drear and dying sound
    Affrights the Flamens at their service quaint;
And the chill marble seems to sweat,
While each peculiar power forgoes his wonted seat.

Peor and Baälim
Forsake their temples dim,
    With that twice-battered god of Palestine;
And moonèd Ashtaroth,
Heaven's queen and mother both,
    Now sits not girt with tapers' holy shine;
The Libyc Hammon shrinks his horn,
In vain the Tyrian maids their wounded Thammuz mourn.

And sullen Moloch fled,
Hath left in shadows dread
    His burning idol all of blackest hue;
In vain with cymbals' ring
They call the grisly king,
    In dismal dance about the furnace blue;
The brutish gods of Nile as fast,
Isis and Orus, and the dog Anubis, haste.

Nor is Osiris seen
In Memphian grove or green,

Trampling the unshowered grass with lowings loud;
Nor can he be at rest
Within his sacred chest;
   Nought but profoundest Hell can be his shroud;
In vain, with timbreled anthems dark,
The sable-stolèd sorcerers bear his worshiped ark.

He feels from Juda's land
The dreaded Infant's hand;
   The rays of Bethlehem blind his dusky eyne;
Nor all the gods beside
Longer dare abide,
   Not Typhon, huge, ending in snaky twine:
Our Babe, to show his Godhead true,
Can in his swaddling bands control the damnèd crew.

So, when the sun in bed,
Curtained with cloudy red,
   Pillows his chin upon an orient wave,
The flocking shadows pale
Troop to the infernal jail,
   Each fettered ghost slips to his several grave,
And the yellow-skirted fays
Fly after the night-steeds, leaving their moon-loved maze.

But see! the Virgin blest
Hath laid her Babe to rest.
   Time is our tedious song should here have ending:
Heaven's youngest-teemèd star
Hath fixed her polished car,
   Her sleeping Lord with handmaid lamp attending;
And all about the courtly stable
Bright-harnessed angels sit in order serviceable.

Richard Crashaw

(1612–1649)

A HYMN TO THE NAME AND HONOR OF THE ADMIRABLE SAINT TERESA

Love, thou art absolute sole lord
Of life and death. To prove the word,
We'll now appeal to none of all
Those thy old soldiers, great and tall,
Ripe men of martyrdom, that could reach down,
With strong arms, their triumphant crown;
Such as could with lusty breath
Speak loud into the face of death
Their great Lord's glorious name—to none
Of those whose spacious bosoms spread a throne
For love at large to fill: spare blood and sweat,
And see him take a private seat,
Making his mansion in the mild
And milky soul of a soft child.
   Scarce hath she learned to lisp the name
Of martyr, yet she thinks it shame
Life should so long play with that breath
Which spent can buy so brave a death.
She never undertook to know
What death with love should have to do,
Nor has she e'er yet understood
Why to show love, she should shed blood
Yet though she cannot tell you why,
She can love, and she can die.
   Scarce hath she blood enough to make
A guilty sword blush for her sake;
Yet hath she a heart dares hope to prove
How much less strong is death than love.

Be love but there, let poor six years
Be posed with the maturest fears
Man trembles at, you straight shall find
Love knows no nonage, nor the mind.
'Tis love, not years, nor limbs, that can
Make the martyr or the man.

    Love touched her heart, and lo it beats
High, and burns with such brave heats,
Such thirsts to die, as dares drink up
A thousand cold deaths in one cup.
Good reason, for she breathes all fire.
Her weak breast heaves with strong desire
Of what she may with fruitless wishes
Seek for amongst her mother's kisses.

    Since 'tis not to be had at home
She'll travel for a martyrdom.
No home for her confesses she
But where she may a martyr be.

    She'll to the Moors and trade with them,
For this unvalued diadem.
She'll offer them her dearest breath,
With Christ's name in't, in change for death.
She'll bargain with them, and will give
Them God, teach them how to live
In him; or if they this deny,
For him she'll teach them how to die.
So shall she leave amongst them sown
Her Lord's blood, or at least her own.

    Farewell then, all the world! Adieu!
Teresa is no more for you.
Farewell, all pleasures, sports, and joys,
(Never till now esteemèd toys).
Farewell whatever dear may be,
Mother's arms or father's knee.
Farewell house and farewell home!
She's for the Moors and martyrdom.

    Sweet, not so fast! Lo thy fair spouse

Whom thou seekst with so swift vows,
Calls thee back, and bids thee come,
T'embrace a milder martyrdom.

　　Blest pow'rs forbid thy tender life
Should bleed upon a barb'rous knife;
Or some base hand have pow'r to race
Thy breast's chaste cabinet, and uncase
A soul kept there so sweet. O no,
Wise heav'n will never have it so.
Thou art love's victim and must die
A death more mystical and high.
Into love's arms thou shalt let fall
A still-surviving funeral.
His is the dart must make the death
Whose stroke shall taste thy hallowed breath;
A dart thrice dipped in that rich flame
Which writes thy spouse's radiant name
Upon the roof of heav'n, where aye
It shines, and with a sov'reign ray
Beats bright upon the burning faces
Of souls which in that name's sweet graces
Find everlasting smiles. So rare,
So spiritual, pure, and fair
Must be th'immortal instrument
Upon whose choice point shall be sent
A life so loved. And that there be
Fit executioners for thee,
The fair'st and first-born sons of fire,
Blest seraphim, shall leave their choir
And turn love's soldiers, upon thee
To exercise their archery.

　　O how oft shalt thou complain
Of a sweet and subtle pain!
Of intolerable joys!
Of a death in which who dies
Loves his death, and dies again,
And would forever so be slain!

And lives and dies and knows not why
To live, but that he thus may never leave to die.
   How kindly will thy gentle heart
Kiss the sweetly-killing dart!
And close in thin embraces keep
Those delicious wounds that weep
Balsam to heal themselves with. Thus
When these thy deaths so numerous,
Shall all at last die into one,
And melt thy soul's sweet mansion,
Like a soft lump of incense, hasted
By too hot a fire, and wasted
Into perfuming clouds, so fast
Shalt thou exhale to heav'n at last
In a resolving sigh, and then—
O what? Ask not the tongues of men.
Angels cannot tell. Suffice
Thy self shall feel thine own full joys
And hold them fast forever. There
So soon as thou shalt first appear,
The moon of maiden stars, thy white
Mistress, attended by such bright
Souls as thy shining self, shall come
And in her first ranks make thee room,
Where 'mongst her snowy family
Immortal welcomes wait for thee.
   O what delight, when revealed life shall stand
And teach thy lips heav'n with her hand,
On which thou now maist to thy wishes
Heap up thy consecrated kisses.
What joys shall seize thy soul when she,
Bending her blessed eyes on thee
(Those second smiles of heav'n), shall dart
Her mild rays through thy melting heart!
   Angels, thy old friends, there shall greet thee,
Glad at their own home now to meet thee.
   All thy good works which went before

And waited for thee at the door,
Shall own thee there; and all in one
Weave a constellation
Of crowns, with which the King thy spouse
Shall build up thy triumphant brows.
All thy old woes shall now smile on thee,
And thy pains sit bright upon thee,
All thy sorrows here shall shine,
And thy sufferings be divine.
Tears shall take comfort and turn gems,
And wrongs repent to diadems.
Ev'n thy deaths shall live, and new
Dress the soul that erst they slew.
Thy wounds shall blush to such bright scars
As keep account of the Lamb's wars.

   Those rare works where thou shalt leave writ
Love's noble history, with wit
Taught thee by none but him, while here
They feed our souls, shall clothe thine there.
Each heav'nly word by whose hid flame
Our hard hearts shall strike fire, the same
Shall flourish on thy brows, and be
Both fire to us, and flame to thee—
Whose light shall live bright in thy face
By glory, in our hearts by grace.

   Thou shalt look round about, and see
Thousands of crowned souls throng to be
Themselves thy crown, sons of thy vows,
The virgin-births with which thy sov'reign spouse
Made fruitful thy fair soul. Go now,
And with them all about thee, bow
To him. Put on (he'll say) put on
My rosy love—that thy rich zone
Sparkling with the sacred flames
Of thousand souls, whose happy names
Heav'n keeps upon thy score. (Thy bright
Life brought them first to kiss the light

151

That kindled them to stars.) And so
Thou with the Lamb, thy Lord, shalt go,
And whereso'er he sets his white
Steps, walk with him those ways of light
Which who in death would live to see,
Must learn in life to die like thee.

Anne Bradstreet

(Ca.1612–1672)

THE FLESH AND THE SPIRIT

In secret place where once I stood,
Close by the banks of lacrym flood,
I heard two sisters reason on
Things that are past and things to come.
One Flesh was called, who had her eye
On worldly wealth and vanity;
The other Spirit, who did rear
Her thoughts unto a higher sphere.
"Sister," quote Flesh, "what livest thou on—
Nothing but meditation?
Doth contemplation feed thee, so
Regardlessly to let earth go?
Can speculation satisfy
Notion without reality?
Dost dream of things beyond the moon,
And dost thou hope to dwell there soon?
Hast treasures there laid up in store
That all in the world thou countest poor?
Art fancy sick, or turned a sot,
To catch at shadows which are not?
Come, come, I'll show unto thy sense
Industry hath its recompense.
What canst desire but thou mayst see

True substance in variety?
Dost honor like? Acquire the same,
As some to their immortal fame,
And trophies to thy name erect
Which wearing time shall ne'er deject.
For riches dost thou long full sore?
Behold enough of precious store;
Earth hath more silver, pearls, and gold
Than eyes can see or hands can hold
Affectest thou pleasure? Take thy fill;
Earth hath enough of what you will.
Then let not go what thou mayst find
For things unknown, only in mind."

Spirit. "Be still, thou unregenerate part;
Disturb no more my settled heart,
For I have vowed, and so will do,
Thee as a foe still to pursue,
And combat with thee will and must
Until I see thee laid in the dust.
Sisters we are, yea, twins we be,
Yet deadly feud 'twixt thee and me;
For from one father are we not.
Thou by old Adam wast begot,
But my arise is from above,
Whence my dear Father I do love.
Thou speakest me fair, but hatest me sore;
Thy flattering shows I'll trust no more.
How oft thy slave hast thou me made
When I believed what thou hast said,
And never had more cause of woe
Than when I did what thou bad'st do.
I'll stop mine ears at these thy charms,
And count them for my deadly harms.
Thy sinful pleasures I do hate,
Thy riches are to me no bait,
Thine honors do nor will I love,

For my ambition lies above.
My greatest honor it shall be
When I am victor over thee,
And triumph shall, with laurel head,
When thou my captive shalt be led.
How I do live thou needst not scoff,
For I have meat thou knowest not of:
The hidden manna I do eat,
The word of life it is my meat.
My thoughts do yield me more content
Than can thy hours in pleasure spent.
Nor are they shadows which I catch,
Nor fancies vain at which I snatch,
But reach at things that are so high
Beyond thy dull capacity.
Eternal substance I do see,
With which enrichéd I would be;
Mine eye doth pierce the heavens, and see
What is invisible to thee.
My garments are not silk or gold,
Nor such like trash which earth doth hold,
But royal robes I shall have on,
More glorious than the glistering sun.
My crown not diamonds, pearls, and gold,
But such as angels' heads enfold.
The city where I hope to dwell
There's none on earth can parallel:
The stately walls, both high and strong,
Are made of precious jasper stone;
The gates of pearl both rich and clear,
And angels are for porters there;
The streets thereof transparent gold,
Such as no eye did e'er behold;
A crystal river there doth run,
Which doth proceed from the Lamb's throne;
Of life there are the waters sure,

Which shall remain for ever pure;
Of sun or moon they have no need,
For glory doth from God proceed—
No candle there, nor yet torch-light,
For there shall be no darksome night.
From sickness and infirmity
For evermore they shall be free,
Nor withering age shall e'er come there,
But beauty shall be bright and clear.
This city pure is not for thee,
For things unclean there shall not be.
If I of Heaven may have my fill,
Take thou the world, and all that will."

Angelus Silesius

(1624–1677)

THE SOUL WHEREIN GOD DWELLS

The soul wherein God dwells,
What church could holier be?
Becomes a walking-tent
Of Heavenly majesty.
How far from here to heaven?
Not very far, my friend,
A single, hearty step
Will all the journey end.
Though Christ a thousand times
In Bethlehem be born,
If He's not born in thee,
Thy soul is still forlorn.
The cross on Golgotha
Will never save thy soul:
The cross in thine own heart

Alone can make thee whole.
Hold thou—where runnest thou?
Know heaven is in thee—
Seek'st thou for God elsewhere,
His face thou'lt never see.
Oh, would thy heart but be
A manger for His birth;
God would once more become
A child upon the earth.
Go out, God will go in;
Die thou—and let Him live;
Be not—and He will be;
Wait, and He'll all things give.
O shame, a silk-worm works
And spins till it can fly;
And thou, my soul, wilt still
On thine old earth-clod lie!

Anonymous translation from the German

Henry Vaughan

(1621–1695)

THE RETREAT

Happy those early days, when I
Shined in my angel infancy;
Before I understood this place
Appointed for my second race,
Or taught my soul to fancy aught
But a white, celestial thought;
When yet I had not walked above
A mile or two from my first Love,
And looking back, at that short space,
Could see a glimpse of His bright face;
When on some gilded cloud or flower

My gazing soul would dwell an hour,
And in those weaker glories spy
Some shadows of eternity;
Before I taught my tongue to wound
My conscience with a sinful sound,
Or had the black art to dispense
A several sin to every sense,
But felt through all this fleshly dress
Bright shoots of everlastingness.

  Oh, how I long to travel back,
And tread again that ancient track!
That I might once more reach that plain
Where first I left my glorious train;
From whence the enlightened spirit sees
That shady city of palm trees.
But, ah! my soul with too much stay
Is drunk, and staggers in the way.
Some men a forward motion love;
But I by backward steps would move,
And when this dust falls to the urn,
In that state I came, return.

Juana Inés de la Cruz

(1651–1695)

A SONNET

This trickery of paint which you perceive
With all the finest hues of art enwrought,
Which is false argument of colors taught
By subtle means the senses to deceive—
This by which foolish women would believe
She could undo the evils years have brought
And conquering in the war against time fought
Could triumph over age, and youth retrieve—

Is all a futile ruse that she has tried,
A fragile flower tossed against the wind,
A useless bribe the power of fate to appease,
A silly effort of mistaken pride,
A base desire, and viewed in rightful mind,
Is dust, a corpse, a shade,—is less than these.

Anonymous translation from the Spanish

part five

Neo-Classical Christian Poems

"Each prayer accepted, and each wish resigned. . . ."

The dove as a Christian symbol represents the Holy Spirit. The imagery derives from the description of Jesus' baptism in the Gospels where a dove appeared as a sign of the Holy Spirit.

John Dryden

(1631–1700)

A SONG FOR SAINT CECILIA'S DAY

1

From harmony, from heavenly harmony
    This universal frame began;
     When Nature underneath a heap
      Of jarring atoms lay,
   And could not heave her head,
The tuneful Voice was heard from high,
   "Arise, ye more than dead."
Then cold and hot and moist and dry
    In order to their stations leap,
     And music's power obey,
From harmony, from heavenly harmony
    This universal frame began:
    From harmony to harmony
Through all the compass of the notes it ran,
The diapason closing full in Man.

2

What passion cannot music raise and quell?
    When Jubal struck the corded shell,
His listening brethren stood around,
    And, wondering, on their faces fell
  To worship that celestial sound:
Less than a God they thought there could not dwell
    Within the hollow of that shell,
    That spoke so sweetly and so well.
What passion cannot music raise and quell?

3

The trumpet's loud clangor
    Excites us to arms
With shrill notes of anger
    And mortal alarms.
The double, double, double beat
    Of the thund'ring drum
    Cries "Hark, the foes come;
Charge, charge, 'tis too late to retreat."

4

The soft complaining flute
In dying notes discovers
The woes of hopeless lovers,
Whose dirge is whispered by the warbling lute.

5

Sharp violins proclaim
Their jealous pangs and desperation,
Fury, frantic indignation,
Depth of pains and height of passion,
    For the fair, disdainful dame.

6

But oh! What art can teach,
What human voice can reach,
The sacred organ's praise?
Notes inspiring holy love,
Notes that wing their heavenly ways
To mend the choirs above.

7

Orpheus could lead the savage race,
And trees unrooted left their place,
    Sequaceous of the lyre;
But bright Cecilia raised the wonder higher;
When to her organ vocal breath was given,

An angel heard and straight appeared,
Mistaking earth for heaven.

As from the power of sacred lays
The spheres began to move,
And sung the great Creator's praise
To all the blest above;
So when the last and dreadful hour
This crumbling pageant shall devour,
The trumpet shall be heard on high,
The dead shall live, the living die,
And music shall untune the sky.

Jean Racine

(1639-1699)

From ESTHER (Act 4)

ESTHER   O sovereign King!
I stand here trembling and alone before thee.
In my childhood my father a thousand times told me
How Thou swore a holy covenant,
Creating for Thy Self a holy people. . . .
It pleased Thy love to choose our forefathers
Promising them by Thy Holy Word
An everlasting posterity.
Alas! our ungrateful people have scorned Thy law;
The cherished nation has violated her covenant;
She has repudiated her spouse and her father,
To surrender to other gods an adulterous honour.
Now she serves a foreign master.
But slavery is not enough, they wish to destroy her.
Our proud conquerors insult our tears,
Crediting their gods for victories earned.
And want today with one mortal blow

To abolish Thy Name, Thy people and Thy sanctuary.
Thus can the wicked, after so many miracles,
Destroy the truth of Thy Word,
Seizing the most cherished of Thy gifts,
The Saviour whom Thou hast promised and whom we await!
No, no, do not allow these savage peoples,
Drunk with our blood, to silence the only voices
Which in all the universe sing Thy praises.
Destroy their empty gods!
As for me, whom Thou keepest among the unbelieving,
Thou knowest my hatred of their wanton rites,
That I rank among the most impious
Their table, their feasts, and their libations;
That all this pomp to which I am condemned,
This crown in which I am forced to appear,
These holy days of vanitous sacrifice,
Alone and in secret I trample underfoot;
That to these vain ornaments I prefer ashes,
And have no comfort but the tears Thou see'st me shed.
I have lain awaiting Thy sign,
To dare embrace Thy people's cause.
That moment has come!: True to Thy word,
I go to confront a formidable king.
It is for Thee that I go. Guide then my steps
Before this proud lion who knows Thee not.
Command that upon seeing me his wrath be appeased
And lend to my speech a charm that will please him.
The tempests, winds, and the skies are under Thy care:
Turn then his fury against our enemies!

From the French, by G.-Gabriel Gisondi

164

Jonathan Swift

(1667–1745)

THE DAY OF JUDGMENT

Once, with a whirl of thought oppressed,
I sunk from reverie to rest.
An horrid vision seized my head;
I saw the graves give up their dead!
Jove, armed with terrors, burst the skies,
The thunder roars, the lightning flies!
Confused, amazed, its fate unknown,
The world stands trembling at his throne!
While each pale sinner hangs his head,
Jove, nodding, shook the heavens and said:
"Offending race of human kind,
By nature, custom, learning, blind;
You who through frailty slipped aside,
And you who never fell—through pride;
And you by differing churches shammed,
Who come to see each other damned
(So some folks told you, but they knew
No more of Jove's designs than you)—
The world's mad business now is o'er,
And I resent those pranks no more.
I to such blockheads set my wit!
I damn such fools!—Go, go you're bit."

Isaac Watts

(1674–1719)

WHEN I SURVEY THE WONDROUS CROSS

When I survey the wondrous Cross
On which the Prince of glory died,
My richest gain I count but loss,
And pour contempt on all my pride.

Forbid it, Lord, that I should boast
Save in the Cross of Christ my God;
All the vain things that charm me most,
I sacrifice them to His Blood.

See from His Head, His Hands, His Feet,
Sorrow and love flow mingling down;
Did e'er such love and sorrow meet,
Or thorns compose so rich a crown?

Were the whole real of nature mine,
That were an offering far too small;
Love so amazing, so Divine,
Demands my soul, my life, my all.

To Christ, Who won for sinners grace
By bitter grief and anguish sore,
Be praise from all the ransom'd race
For ever and for evermore.

Alexander Pope

(1688–1744)

ELOISA TO ABELARD

In these deep solitudes and awful cells,
Where heavenly-pensive contemplation dwells,
And ever musing melancholy reigns;
What means this tumult in a Vestal's veins?
Why rove my thoughts beyond this last retreat?
Why feels my heart its long-forgotten heat?
Yet, yet I love!—From Abelard it came,
And Eloisa yet must kiss the name.

    Dear fatal name! rest ever unrevealed,
Nor pass these lips in holy silence sealed:
Hide it, my heart, within that close disguise,
Where, mixed with God's, his loved Idea lies:
O write it not, my hand—The name appears
Already written—wash it out, my tears!
In vain lost Eloisa weeps and prays,
Her heart still dictates, and her hand obeys.

    Relentless walls! whose darksome round contains
Repentant sighs and voluntary pains;
Ye rugged rocks! which holy knees have worn;
Ye grots and caverns shagged with horrid thorn!
Shrines! where their vigils pale-eyed virgins keep,
And pitying saints, whose statues learn to weep!
Though cold like you, unmoved and silent grown,
I have not yet forgot myself to stone.
All is not Heaven's while Abelard has part,
Still rebel nature holds out half my heart;
Nor prayers nor fasts its stubborn pulse restrain,
Nor tears, for ages taught to flow in vain.

    Soon as thy letters trembling I unclose,
That well-known name awakens all my woes.

Oh name forever sad! forever dear!
Still breathed in sighs, still ushered with a tear.
I tremble too, where-e'er my own I find,
Some dire misfortune follows close behind.
Line after line my gushing eyes o'erflow
Led through a sad variety of woe:
Now warm in love, now withering in Thy bloom,
Lost in a convent's solitary gloom!
There stern religion quenched the unwilling flame,
There died the best of passions, Love and Fame.

Yet write, oh write me all, that I may join
Griefs to thy griefs, and echo sighs to thine.
Nor foes nor fortune take this power away,
And is my Abelard less kind than they?
Tears still are mine, and those I need not spare,
Love but demands what else were shed in prayer;
No happier task these faded eyes pursue,
To read and weep is all they now can do.

Then share thy pain, allow that sad relief;
Ah more than share it! give me all thy grief.
Heaven first taught letters for some wretch's aid,
Some banished lover, or some captive maid;
They live, they speak, they breathe what love inspires,
Warm from the soul, and faithful to its fires,
The virgin's wish without her fears impart,
Excuse the blush, and pour out all the heart,
Speed the soft intercourse from soul to soul,
And waft a sigh from Indus to the Pole.

Thou know'st how guiltless first I met thy flame,
When Love approached me under Friendship's name;
My fancy formed thee of angelic kind,
Some emanation of the all-beauteous Mind
Those smiling eyes, attempering every ray,
Shone sweetly lambent with celestial day:
Guiltless I gazed; Heaven listened while you sung;
And truths divine came mended from that tongue.
From lips like those what precept failed to move?
Too soon they taught me 'twas no sin to love.

Back through the paths of pleasing sense I ran,
Nor wished an angel whom I loved a man.
Dim and remote the joys of saints I see,
Nor envy them that heaven I lose for thee.
    How oft, when pressed to marriage, have I said,
Curse on all laws but those which love has made!
Love, free as air, at sight of human ties,
Spreads his light wings, and in a moment flies.
Let wealth, let honour, wait the wedded dame,
August her deed, and sacred be her fame;
Before true passion all those views remove,
Fame, wealth, and honour! what are you to Love?
The jealous God, when we profane his fires,
Those restless passions in revenge inspires;
And bids them make mistaken mortals groan,
Who seek in love for aught but love alone.
Should at my feet the world's great master fall,
Himself, his throne, his world, I'd scorn 'em all:
Not Caesar's empress would I deign to prove;
No, make me mistress to the man I love;
If there be yet another name more free,
More fond than mistress, make me that to thee!
Oh happy state! when souls each other draw,
When love is liberty, and nature law:
All then is full, possessing, and possessed,
No craving void left aching in the breast:
Even thought meets thought, ere from the lips it part,
And each warm wish springs mutual from the heart.
This sure is bliss (if bliss on earth there be)
And once the lot of Abelard and me.
    Alas how changed! what sudden horrors rise!
A naked lover bound and bleeding lies!
Where, where was Eloise? her voice, her hand,
Her poniard, had opposed the dire command.
Barbarian stay! that bloody stroke restrain;
The crime was common, common be the pain.
I can no more; by shame, by rage suppressed,
Let tears and burning blushes speak the rest.

Canst thou forget that sad, that solemn day,
When victims at yon' altar's foot we lay?
Canst thou forget what tears that moment fell,
When, warm in youth, I bade the world farewell?
As with cold lips I kissed the sacred veil,
The shrines all trembled, and the lamps grew pale:
Heaven scarce believed the conquest it surveyed,
And saints with wonder heard the vows I made.
Yet then, to those dread altars as I drew,
Not on the Cross my eyes were fixed, but you:
Not grace, or zeal, love only was my call,
And if I lose thy love, I lose my all.
Come! with thy looks, thy words, relieve my woe;
Those still at least are left thee to bestow.
Still on that breast enamoured let me lie,
Still drink delicious poison from thy eye,
Pant on thy lip, and to thy heart be pressed;
Give all thou canst—and let me dream the rest.
Ah no! instruct me other joys to prize,
With other beauties charm my partial eyes,
Full in my view set all the bright abode,
And make my soul quit Abelard for God.

  Ah think at least thy flock deserves thy care,
Plants of thy hand, and children of thy prayer.
From the false world in early youth they fled,
By thee to mountains, wilds, and deserts led.
You raised these hallowed walls; the desert smiled,
And Paradise was opened in the wild.
No weeping orphan saw his father's stores
Our shrines irradiate, or emblaze the floors:
No silver saints, by dying misers given,
Here bribed the rage of ill-requited Heaven:
But such plain roofs as piety could raise,
And only vocal with the Maker's praise.
In these lone walls (their days eternal bound)
These moss-grown domes with spiry turrets crowned,
Where awful arches make a noonday night,
And the dim windows shed a solemn light;

Thy eyes diffused a reconciling ray,
And gleams of glory brightened all the day.
But now no face divine contentment wears,
'Tis all blank sadness, or continual tears.
See how the force of others' prayers I try,
(O pious fraud of amorous charity!)
But why should I on others' prayers depend?
Come thou, my father, brother, husband, friend!
Ah let thy handmaid, sister, daughter, move,
And all those tender names in one, thy love!
The darksome pines that o'er yon rocks reclined
Wave high, and murmur to the hollow wind,
The wandering streams that shine between the hills,
The grots that echo to the tinkling rills,
The dying gales that pant upon the trees,
The lakes that quiver to the curling breeze;
No more these scenes my meditation aid,
Or lull to rest the visionary maid.
But o'er the twilight groves and dusky caves,
Long-sounding isles, and intermingled graves,
Black Melancholy sits, and round her throws
A death-like silence, and a dead repose:
Her gloomy presence saddens all the scene,
Shades every flower, and darkens every green,
Deepens the murmur of the falling floods,
And breathes a browner horror on the woods.

   Yet here forever, ever must I stay;
Sad proof how well a lover can obey!
Death, only death, can break the lasting chain;
And here, even then, shall my cold dust remain,
Here all its frailties, all its flames resign,
And wait till 'tis no sin to mix with thine.

   Ah wretch! believed the spouse of God in vain,
Confessed within the slave of love and man.
Assist me Heaven! but whence arose that prayer?
Sprung it from piety, or from despair?
Even here, where frozen chastity retires,
Love finds an altar for forbidden fires.

I ought to grieve, but cannot what I ought;
I mourn the lover, not lament the fault;
I view my crime, but kindle at the view,
Repent old pleasures, and solicit new;
Now turned to Heaven, I weep my past offence,
Now think of thee, and curse my innocence.
Of all affliction taught a lover yet,
'Tis sure the hardest science to forget!
How shall I lose the sin, yet keep the sense,
And love the offender, yet detest the offence?
How the dear object from the crime remove,
Or how distinguish penitence from love?
Unequal task! a passion to resign,
For hearts so touched, so pierced, so lost as mine.
Ere such a soul regains its peaceful state,
How often must it love, how often hate!
How often, hope, despair, resent, regret,
Conceal, disdain,—do all things but forget.
But let Heaven seize it, all at once 'tis fired:
Not touched, but rapt; not wakened, but inspired!
Oh come! oh teach me nature to subdue,
Renounce my love, my life, myself—and you.
Fill my fond heart with God alone, for he
Alone can rival, can succeed to thee.

How happy is the blameless Vestal's lot!
The world forgetting, by the world forgot:
Eternal sunshine of the spotless mind!
Each prayer accepted, and each wish resigned;
Labour and rest, that equal periods keep;
'Obedient slumbers that can wake and weep';
Desires composed, affections ever even;
Tears that delight, and sighs that waft to Heaven.
Grace shines around her with serenest beams,
And whispering angels prompt her golden dreams.
For her the unfading rose of Eden blooms,
And wings of seraphs shed divine perfumes;
For her the Spouse prepares the bridal ring,
For her white virgins hymeneals sing,

To sounds of heavenly harps she dies away,
And melts in visions of eternal day.

Far other dreams my erring soul employ,
Far other raptures, of unholy joy:
When at the close of each sad, sorrowing day,
Fancy restores what vengeance snatched away,
Then conscience sleeps, and leaving nature free,
All my loose soul unbounded springs to thee.
Oh curst, dear horrors of all-conscious night;
How glowing guilt exalts the keen delight!
Provoking demons all restraint remove,
And stir within me every source of love.
I hear thee, view thee, gaze o'er all thy charms,
And round thy phantom glue my clasping arms.
I wake—no more I hear, no more I view,
The phantom flies me, as unkind as you.
I call aloud; it hears not what I say:
I stretch my empty arms; it glides away.
To dream once more I close my willing eyes;
Ye soft illusions, dear deceits, arise!
Alas no more! methinks we wandering go
Through dreary wastes, and weep each other's woe,
Where round some mouldering tower pale ivy creeps,
And low-browed rocks hang nodding o'er the deeps.
Sudden you mount! you beckon from the skies;
Clouds interpose, waves roar, and winds arise.
I shriek, start up, the same sad prospect find,
And wake to all the griefs I left behind.

For thee the fates, severely kind, ordain
A cool suspense from pleasure and from pain;
Thy life a long dead calm of fixed repose;
No pulse that riots, and no blood that glows,
Still as the sea, ere winds were taught to blow,
Or moving spirit bade the waters flow;
Soft as the slumbers of a saint forgiven,
And mild as opening gleams of promised Heaven.

Come Abelard! for what hast thou to dread?
The torch of Venus burns not for the dead.

Nature stands checked; Religion disapproves;
Even thou art cold—yet Eloisa loves.
Ah hopeless, lasting flames! like those that burn
To light the dead, and warm the unfruitful urn.

What scenes appear where'er I turn my view!
The dear ideas, where I fly, pursue,
Rise in the grove, before the altar rise,
Stain all my soul, and wanton in my eyes.
I waste the matin lamp in sighs for thee,
Thy image steals between my God and me,
Thy voice I seem in every hymn to hear,
With every bead I drop too soft a tear.
When from the censer clouds of fragrance roll,
And swelling organs lift the rising soul,
One thought of thee puts all the pomp to flight,
Priests, tapers, temples, swim before my sight:
In seas of flame my plunging soul is drowned,
While altars blaze, and angels tremble round.

While prostrate here in humble grief I lie,
Kind, virtuous drops just gathering in my eye,
While praying, trembling, in the dust I roll,
And dawning grace is opening on my soul:
Come, if thou darest, all charming as thou art!
Oppose thyself to Heaven; dispute my heart;
Come, with one glance of those deluding eyes
Blot out each bright idea of the skies;
Take back that grace, those sorrows, and those tears;
Take back my fruitless penitence and prayers;
Snatch me, just mounting, from the blest abode;
Assist the fiends, and tear me from my God!

No, fly me, fly me, far as Pole from Pole;
Rise Alps between us! and whole oceans roll!
Ah come not, write not, think not once of me,
Nor share one pang of all I felt for thee.
Thy oaths I quit, thy memory resign;
Forget, renounce me, hate whate'er was mine.
Fair eyes, and tempting looks (which yet I view!)
Long loved, adored ideas, all adieu!

Oh Grace serene! oh virtue heavenly fair!
Divine oblivion of low-thoughted care!
Fresh blooming Hope, gay daughter of the sky!
And Faith, our early immortality!
Enter, each mild, each amicable guest;
Receive, and wrap me in eternal rest!
   See in her cell sad Eloisa spread,
Propped on some tomb, a neighbour of the dead!
In each low wind methinks a spirit calls,
And more than echoes talk along the walls.
Here, as I watched the dying lamps around,
From yonder shrine I heard a hollow sound.
Come, sister, come! it said, or seemed to say,
Thy place is here, sad sister, come away!
Once like thyself, I trembled, wept, and prayed,
Love's victim then, though now a sainted maid:
But all is calm in this eternal sleep:
Here grief forgets to groan, and love to weep;
Even superstition loses every fear,
For God, not man, absolves our frailties here.
   I come, I come! prepare your roseate bowers,
Celestial palms, and ever-blooming flowers.
Thither, where sinners may have rest, I go,
Where flames refined in breasts seraphic glow:
Thou, Abelard! the last sad office pay,
And smooth my passage to the realms of day;
See my lips tremble, and my eyeballs roll,
Suck my last breath, and catch my flying soul!
Ah no—in sacred vestments may'st thou stand,
The hallowed taper trembling in thy hand,
Present the Cross before my lifted eye,
Teach me at once, and learn of me to die.
Ah then, thy once loved Eloisa see!
It will be then no crime to gaze on me.
See from my cheek the transient roses fly!
See the last sparkle languish in my eye!
Till every motion, pulse, and breath be o'er;
And even my Abelard be loved no more.

O Death all-eloquent! you only prove
What dust we dote on, when 'tis man we love,
   Then too, when fate shall thy fair frame destroy,
(That cause of all my guilt, and all my joy)
In trance ecstatic may thy pangs be drowned,
Bright clouds descend, and angels watch thee round,
From opening skies may streaming glories shine,
And saints embrace thee with a love like mine.
May one kind grave unite each hapless name,
And graft my love immortal on thy fame!
Then, ages hence, when all my woes are o'er,
When this rebellious heart shall beat no more;
If ever chance two wandering lovers brings
To Paraclete's white walls and silver springs,
O'er the pale marble shall they join their heads,
And drink the falling tears each other sheds;
Then sadly say, with mutual pity moved,
Oh may we never love as these have loved!
From the full choir when loud hosannas rise,
And swell the pomp of dreadful sacrifice,
Amid that scene if some relenting eye
Glance on the stone where our cold relics lie,
Devotion's self shall steal a thought from Heaven,
One human tear shall drop and be forgiven.
And sure, if fate some future bard shall join
In sad similitude of griefs to mine,
Condemned whole years in absence to deplore,
And image charms he must behold no more;
Such if there be, who loves so long, so well,
Let him our sad, our tender story tell;
The well-sung woes will soothe my pensive ghost;
He best can paint 'em who shall feel 'em most.

Christopher Smart

(1722–1791)

From A SONG TO DAVID

Tell them I am, Jehovah said
To Moses; while earth heard in dread,
   And smitten to the heart,
At one above, beneath, around,
All nature, without voice or sound,
   Replied, O Lord, THOU ART.

Thou art—to give and to confirm,
For each his talent and his term;
   All flesh thy bounties share:
Thou shalt not call thy brother fool;
The porches of the Christian school
   Are meekness, peace, and pray'r.

Open, and naked of offence,
Man's made of mercy, soul and sense;
   God armed the snail and wilk;
Be good to him that pulls thy plough;
Due food and care, due rest, allow
   For her that yields thee milk.

Rise up before the hoary head,
And God's benign commandment dread,
   Which says thou shalt not die:
'Not as I will, but as thou wilt,'
Prays He whose conscience knew no guilt;
   With whose bless'd pattern vie.

William Cowper

(1731–1800)

THE BLOOD OF CHRIST

There is a fountain fill'd with Blood,
   Drawn from Emmanuel's veins,
And sinners plunged beneath that flood
   Lose all their guilty stains.

The dying thief rejoiced to see
   That fountain in his day;
And there may I, as vile as he,
   Wash all my sins away.

Dear dying Lamb, Thy precious Blood
   Shall never lose its power,
Till all the ransom'd Church of God
   Be saved to sin no more.

Ever since by faith I saw the stream
   Thy flowing wounds supply,
Redeeming love has been my theme,
   And shall be till I die.

Then in a nobler, sweeter song,
   I'll sing Thy power to save,
When this poor lisping, stammering tongue
   Lies silent in the grave.

Lord, I believe Thou hast prepared,
   Unworthy though I be,
For me a blood-bought free reward,
   A golden harp for me.

'Tis strung and tuned for endless years,
   And form'd by power divine,
To sound in God the Father's ears
   No other name but Thine.

part six

Romantic Christian Poems

"This life's dim windows of the soul."

The lamb, one of the earliest Christian symbols, usually represents Christ as Savior though it can also symbolize the Christian soul tended by the Good Shepherd. The lamb as a sacrificial animal is noted throughout the Bible.

Charles Wesley

(1707–1788)

A MORNING HYMN

Christ, whose glory fills the skies,
  Christ, the true, the only Light,
Sun of Righteousness, arise,
  Triumph o'er the shades of night:
Dayspring from on high, be near;
Daystar, in my heart appear.

Dark and cheerless is the morn,
  Unaccompanied by Thee;
Joyless is the day's return,
  Till Thy mercy's beams I see;
Till thy inward light impart,
Glad my eyes, and warm my heart.

Visit then this soul of mine;
  Pierce the gloom of sin and grief;
Fill me, Radiancy divine;
  Scatter all my unbelief:
More and more Thyself display,
Shining to the perfect Day.

Friedrich Gottlieb Klopstock

(1724–1803)

HOW THEY SO SOFTLY REST

How they so softly rest,
All, all the holy dead,
Unto whose dwelling place
Now doth my soul draw near!
How they so softly rest,
All in their silent graves,
Deep to corruption
Slowly down-sinking!

And they no longer weep,
Here, where complaint is still!
And they no longer feel,
Here, where all gladness flies!
And, by the cypresses
Softly o'ershadowed,
Until the Angel
Calls them, they slumber!

From the German, by Henry W. Longfellow

William Blake

(1757–1827)

THE EVERLASTING GOSPEL

Was Jesus Humble or did he
Give any Proofs of Humility
Boast of high Things with Humble tone
And give with Charity a Stone

When but a Child he ran away
And left his Parents in dismay
When they had wandered three days long
These were the words upon his tongue
No Earthly Parents I confess
I am doing my Fathers business
When the rich learned Pharisee
Came to consult him secretly
Upon his heart with Iron pen
He wrote Ye must be born again
He was too proud to take a bribe
He spoke with authority not like a Scribe
He says with most consummate Art
Follow me I am meek & lowly of heart
As that is the only way to escape
The Misers net & the Gluttons trap
What can be done with such desperate Fools
Who follow after the Heathen Schools
I was standing by when Jesus died
What I calld Humility they calld Pride
He who loves his Enemies betrays his Friends
This surely is not what Jesus intends
But the sneaking Pride of Heroic Schools
And the Scribes & Pharisees Virtuous Rules
For he acts with honest triumphant Pride
And this is the cause that Jesus died
He did not die with Christian Ease
Asking pardon of his Enemies
If he had Caiaphas would forgive
Sneaking submission can always live
He had only to say that God was the devil
And the devil was God like a Christian Civil
Mild Christian regrets to the devil confess
For affronting him thrice in the Wilderness
He had soon been bloody Caesars Elf
And at last he would have been Caesar himself
Like d^r Priestly & Bacon & Newton
Poor Spiritual Knowledge is not worth a button

For thus the Gospel Sr Isaac confutes
God can only be known by his Attributes
And as for the Indwelling of the Holy Ghost
Or of Christ & his Father its all a boast
And Pride & Vanity of the imagination
That disdains to follow this Worlds Fashion
To teach doubt & Experiment
Certainly was not what Christ meant
What was he doing all that time
From twelve years old to manly prime
Was he then Idle or the Less
About his Fathers business
Or was his wisdom held in scorn
Before his wrath began to burn
In Miracles throughout the Land
That quite unnervd Caiaphas hand
If he had been Antichrist Creeping Jesus
Hed have done any thing to please us
Gone sneaking into Synagogues
And not usd the Elders & Priests like dogs
But Humble as a Lamb or Ass
Obeyd himself to Caiaphas
God wants not Man to Humble himself
This is the trick of the ancient Elf
This is the Race that Jesus ran
Humble to God Haughty to Man
Cursing the Rulers before the People
Even to the temples highest Steeple
And when he Humbled himself to God
Then descended the Cruel Rod
If thou humblest thyself thou humblest me
Thou also dwellst in Eternity
Thou art a Man God is no more
Thy own humanity learn to adore
For that is my Spirit of Life
Awake arise to Spiritual Strife
And thy Revenge abroad display
In terrors at the Last Judgment day

184

Gods Mercy & Long Suffering
Is but the Sinner to Judgment to bring
Thou on the Cross for them shalt pray
And take Revenge at the Last Day
Jesus replied & thunders hurld
I never will Pray for the World
Once [I] did so when I prayd in the Garden
I wishd to take with me a Bodily Pardon
Can that which was of woman born
In the absence of the Morn
When the Soul fell into Sleep
And Archangels round it weep
Shooting out against the Light
Fibres of a deadly night
Reasoning upon its own dark Fiction
In doubt which is Self Contradiction
Humility is only doubt
And does the Sun & Moon blot out
Rooting over with thorns & stems
The buried Soul & all its Gems.
This Lifes dim Windows of the Soul
Distorts the Heavens from Pole to Pole
And leads you to Believe a Lie
When you see with not thro the Eye
That was born in a night to perish in a night
When the Soul slept in the beams of Light.
Was Jesus Chaste or did he
Give any Lessons of Chastity
The morning blushd fiery red
Mary was found in Adulterous bed
Earth groand beneath & Heaven above
Trembled at discovery of Love
Jesus was sitting in Moses Chair
They brought the trembling Woman There
Moses commands she be stoned to death
What was the sound of Jesus breath
He laid His hand on Moses Law
The Ancient Heavens in Silent Awe

Writ with Curses from Pole to Pole
All away began to roll
The Earth trembling & Naked lay
In secret bed of Mortal Clay
On Sinai felt the hand Divine
Putting back the bloody shrine
And she heard the breath of God
As she heard by Edens flood
Good & Evil are no more
Sinais trumpets cease to roar
Cease finger of God to write
The Heavens are not clean in thy Sight
Thou art Good & thou Alone
Nor may the sinner cast one stone
To be Good only is to be
A God or else a Pharisee
Thou Angel of the Presence Divine
That didst create this Body of Mine
Wherefore has thou writ these Laws
And Created Hells dark jaws
My Presence I will take from thee
A Cold Leper thou shalt be
Tho thou wast so pure & bright
That Heaven was Impure in thy Sight
Tho thy Oath turnd Heaven Pale
Tho thy Covenant built Hells Jail
Tho thou didst all to Chaos roll
With the Serpent for its soul
Still the breath Divine does move
And the breath Divine is Love
Mary Fear Not Let me see
The Seven Devils that torment thee
Hide not from my Sight thy Sin
That forgiveness thou maist win
Has no Man Condemned thee
No Man Lord! then what is he
Who shall Accuse thee. Come Ye forth
Fallen Fiends of Heavnly birth

That have forgot your Ancient love
And driven away my trembling Dove
You shall bow before her feet
You shall lick the dust for Meat
And tho you cannot Love but Hate
Shall be beggars at Loves Gate
What was thy love Let me see it
Was it love or Dark Deceit
Love too long from Me has fled.
Twas dark deceit to Earn my bread
Twas Covet or twas Custom or
Some trifle not worth caring for
That they may call a shame & Sin
Loves temple that God dwelleth in
And hide in secret hidden Shrine
The Naked Human form divine
And render that a Lawless thing
On which the Soul Expands its wing
But this O Lord this was my Sin
When first I let these Devils in
In dark pretence to Chastity
Blaspheming Love blaspheming thee
Thence Rose Secret Adulteries
And thence did Covet also rise
My sin thou hast forgiven me
Canst thou forgive my Blasphemy
Canst thou return to this dark Hell
And in my burning bosom dwell
And canst thou die that I may live
And canst thou Pity & forgive
Then Rolld the shadowy Man away
From the Limbs of Jesus to make them his prey
An Ever devo[u]ring appetite
Glittering with festering Venoms bright
Crying Crucify this cause of distress
Who dont keep the secrets of Holiness
All Mental Powers by Diseases we bind
But he heals the Deaf & the Dumb & the Blind

Whom God has afflicted for Secret Ends
He comforts & Heals & calls them Friends
But when Jesus was Crucified
Then was perfected his glittring pride
In three Nights he devourd his prey
And still he devours the Body of Clay
For dust & Clay is the Serpents meat
Which never was made for Man to Eat
Was Jesus gentle or did he
Give any marks of Gentility
When twelve years old he ran away
And left his Parents in dismay
When after three days sorrow found
Loud as Sinai's trumpet sound
No Earthly Parents I confess
My Heavenly Fathers business
Ye understand not what I say
And angry force me to obey
Obedience is a duty then
And favour gains with God & Men
John from the Wilderness loud cried
Satan gloried in his Pride
Come said Satan come away
Ill soon see if youll obey
John for disobedience bled
But you can turn the stones to bread
Gods high king & Gods high Priest
Shall Plant their Glories in your breast
If Caiaphas you will obey
If Herod you with bloody Prey
Feed with the Sacrifice & be
Obedient fall down worship me
Thunders & lightnings broke around
And Jesus voice in thunders sound
Thus I sieze the Spiritual Prey
Ye smiters with disease make way
I come Your King & God to sieze
Is God a Smiter with disease

The God of this World raged in vain
He bound Old Satan in his Chain
And bursting forth his furious ire
Became a Chariot of fire
Throughout the land he took his course
And traced diseases to their source
He cursd the Scribe & Pharisee
Trampling down Hipocrisy
Where eer his Chariot took its way
There Gates of Death let in the day
Broke down from every Chain & Bar
And Satan in his Spiritual War
Dragd at his Chariot wheels loud howld
The God of this World louder rolld
The Chariot Wheels & louder still
His voice was heard from Zions hill
And in his hand the Scourge shone bright
He scourgd the Merchant Canaanite
From out the Temple of his Mind
And in his Body tight does bind
Satan & all his Hellish Crew
And thus with wrath he did subdue
The Serpent Bulk of Natures dross
Till he had naild it to the Cross
He took on Sin in the Virgins Womb
And put it off on the Cross & Tomb
To be Worshipd by the Church of Rome
The Vision of Christ that thou dost see
Is my Visions Greatest Enemy
Thine has a great hook nose like thine
Mine has a snub nose like to mine
Thine is the friend of All Mankind
Mine speaks in parables to the Blind
Thine loves the same world that mine hates
Thy Heaven doors are my Hell Gates
Socrates taught what Melitus
Loathd as a Nations bitterest Curse
And Caiaphas was in his own Mind

A benefactor to Mankind
Both read the Bible day & night
But thou readst black where I read white

Novalis

(1772–1801)

WHEN SADNESS AND WEARINESS

When sadness and weariness
    cast their shadows over us;
And the power of sickness eats
    away at our inmost soul:
When we think of one we love,
    suffering with pain and grief;
The very heavens then become
    clouded and all hope useless.

God then bends down to comfort us,
    His love draws near:
If we wish for death to free us,
    He sends an angel with
The cup of Life, restoring and
    giving strength from Heaven.
Our prayers are not in vain, He
    sends peaceful rest for those we love.

From the German, by Ronald J. Suter

Esaias Tegnér

(1782–1846)

From THE CHILDREN OF THE LORD'S SUPPER

Love is life, but hatred is death. Not father, nor mother
Loved you, as God has loved you; for 't was that you may be happy
Gave he his only Son. When he bowed down his head in the death-hour
Solemnized Love its triumph; the sacrifice then was completed.
Lo! then was rent on a sudden the veil of the temple, dividing
Earth and heaven apart, and the dead from their sepulchres rising
Whispered with pallid lips and low in the ears of each other
Th' answer, but dreamed of before, to creation's enigma—Atonement!
Depths of Love are Atonement's depths, for Love is Atonement.

From the Swedish, by Henry W. Longfellow

Clemens Brentano

(1778–1842)

LORD! ONLY IN YOUR PEACE CAN I FIND REST

Lord! Only in your peace can I find rest,
    whether I desire to live or die:
Here on earth my Saviour died
    that I might inherit everlasting Life.

The butterfly seeks the sunlight,
    breaking its woven house:
Now, my body is being destroyed
    that I too may find my freedom.

Lord, grant me such a death
    when my life has reached its end.

191

Give me a clear mind so I may
   return my soul to your keeping.

Within your hands are the hearts of
   the humble which glow before You
Like children in their cradles,
   quietly sleeping, untouched by grief.

From the German, by Ronald J. Suter

Alphonse Marie Louis de Lamartine

(1792–1869)

From ENCORE UN HYMNE, O MA LYRE!

O Thou who bidst the torrent flow,
   Who lendest wings unto the wind,—
Mover of all things! where art Thou?
   Oh, whither shall I go to find
The secret of Thy resting-place?
   Is there no holy wing for me,
That, soaring, I may search the space
   Of highest heaven for Thee?

Oh, would I were as free to rise
   As leaves on autumn's whirlwind borne,—
The arrowy light of sunset skies,
   Or sound, or ray, or star of morn,
Which melts in heaven at twilight's close,
   Or aught which soars unchecked and free
Through earth and heaven; that I might lose
   Myself in finding Thee!

From the French, by John Greenleaf Whittier

William Cullen Bryant

(1794–1878)

HYMN OF THE WALDENSES

Hear, Father, hear thy faint afflicted flock
Cry to thee, from the desert and the rock;
While those, who seek to slay thy children, hold
Blasphemous worship under roofs of gold;
And the broad goodly lands, with pleasant airs
That nurse the grape and wave the grain, are theirs.

Yet better were this mountain wilderness,
And this wild life of danger and distress—
Watchings by night and perilous flight by day,
And meetings in the depths of earth to pray,
Better, far better, than to kneel with them,
And pay the impious rite thy laws condemn.

Thou, Lord, dost hold the thunder; the firm land
Tosses in billows when it feels thy hand;
Thou dashest nation against nation, then
Stillest the angry world to peace again.
Oh, touch their stony hearts who hunt thy sons—
The murderers of our wives and little ones.

Yet, mighty God, yet shall thy frown look forth
Unveiled, and terribly shall shake the earth.
Then the foul power of priestly sin and all
Its long-upheld idolatries shall fall.
Thou shalt raise up the trampled and oppressed,
And thy delivered saints shall dwell in rest.

Adam Mickiewicz

(1798–1855)

SPIN LOVE

Spin love, spin love out of your heart
　　As from the worm the silk is wound,
As from the spring the waters start,
　　As flows the river underground.
Unroll love like those glittering sheets,
　　Papyrus-thin, and bright with glamor,
Which patiently the goldsmith beats
　　Out of an ingot with a hammer.
And blow love as the zephyr blows,
　　Upward and outward, far and wide,
And cast it as the farmer sows
　　The prodigal grain on every side.
Love men and women everywhere,
　　All human creatures brought to birth,
As mothers for their children care.
　　Your hands will have more power on earth
Than nature has; and then your strength,
　　Indomitable, shall equate
That of the elements, and, at length,
　　Shall be the power to propagate,
Then be the power of the people,
　　Then power of a heavenly hoarde
Of angels flying round a steeple—
　　At last, the power of the Lord.

From the Polish, by Kimball Flaccus

part seven

Victorian Christian Poems

"All we have willed or hoped or dreamed of good shall exist . . .."

The eagle was believed to renew its youth by flying near the sun and then diving near the water, and came to be used as a symbol of the Resurrection. It also serves as a symbol for the Gospel According to John, since it "soars to heavenly heights," according to Augustine.

Henry Wadsworth Longfellow

(1807–1882)

SONNET ONE: ON THE DIVINA COMMEDIA

Oft have I seen at some cathedral door
  A laborer, pausing in the dust and heat,
  Lay down his burden, and with reverent feet
  Enter, and cross himself, and on the floor
Kneel to repeat his paternoster o'er;
  Far off the noises of the world retreat;
  The loud vociferations of the street
  Become an undistinguishable roar.
So, as I enter here from day to day,
And leave my burden at the minster gate,
Kneeling in prayer, and not ashamed to pray,
The tumult of the time disconsolate
  To inarticulate murmurs dies away,
  While the eternal ages watch and wait.

John Greenleaf Whittier

(1807–1892)

LAUS DEO!

*On Hearing the Bells Ring on the Passage of
the Constitutional Amendment Abolishing Slavery*

It is done!
    Clang of bell and roar of gun
Send the tidings up and down.
    How the belfries rock and reel!
    How the great guns, peal on peal,
Fling the joy from town to town!

    Ring, O Bells!
    Every stroke exulting tells
Of the burial hour of crime
    Loud and long, that all may hear,
    Ring for every listening ear
Of Eternity and Time!

    Let us kneel:
    God's own voice is in that peal,
And this spot is holy ground.
    Lord, forgive us! What are we,
    That our eyes this glory see,
That our ears have heard the sound!

    For the Lord
    On the whirlwind is abroad;
In the earthquake he has spoken;
    He has smitten with his thunder
    The iron walls asunder,
And the gates of brass are broken!

    Loud and long
    Lift the old exulting song;
Sing with Miriam by the sea
    He has cast the mighty down;
    Horse and rider sink and drown;
"He hath triumphed gloriously!"

    Did we dare,
    In our agony of prayer,
Ask for more than He has done?
    When was ever his right hand

Over any time or land
Stretched as now beneath the sun?

How they pale,
Ancient myth and song and tale,
In this wonder of our days,
When the cruel rod of war
Blossoms white with righteous law,
And the wrath of man is praise!

Blotted out!
All within and all about
Shall a fresher life begin;
Freer breathe the universe
As it rolls its heavy curse
On the dead and buried sin!

It is done!
In the circuit of the sun
Shall the sound thereof go forth.
It shall bid the sad rejoice,
It shall give the dumb a voice,
It shall belt with joy the earth!

Ring and swing,
Bells of joy! On the morning's wing
Send the song of praise abroad!
With the sound of broken chains
Tell the nations that He reigns
Who alone is Lord and God!

Alfred Tennyson

(1809–1892)

From IN MEMORIAM

Strong Son of God, immortal Love,
    Whom we, that have not seen thy face,
    By faith, and faith alone embrace,
Believing where we cannot prove;

Thine are these orbs of light and shade;
    Thou madest Life in man and brute;
    Thou madest Death; and lo, thy foot
Is on the skull which thou hast made.

Thou wilt not leave us in the dust:
    Thou madest man, he knows not why,
    He thinks he was not made to die;
And thou hast made him: thou art just.

Thou seemest human and divine,
    The highest, holiest manhood, thou.
    Our wills are ours, we know not how;
Our wills are ours, to make them thine.

Our little systems have their day;
    They have their day and cease to be;
    They are but broken lights of thee,
And thou, O Lord, art more than they.

We have but faith: we cannot know,
    For knowledge is of things we see;
    And yet we trust it comes from thee,
A beam in darkness: let it grow.

Let knowledge grow from more to more,
    But more of reverence in us dwell;

That mind and soul, according well,
May make one music as before,

But vaster. We are fools and slight;
   We mock thee when we do not fear:
   But help thy foolish ones to bear;
Help thy vain worlds to bear thy light.

Forgive what seemed my sin in me,
   What seemed my worth since I began;
   For merit lives from man to man,
And not from man, O Lord, to thee.

Forgive my grief for one removed,
   Thy creature, whom I found so fair.
   I trust he lives in thee, and there
I find him worthier to be loved.

Forgive these wild and wandering cries,
   Confusions of a wasted youth;
   Forgive them where they fail in truth,
And in thy wisdom make me wise.

I

I held it truth, with him who sings
   To one clear harp in divers tones,
   That men may rise on stepping-stones
Of their dead selves to higher things.

But who shall so forecast the years
   And find in loss a gain to match?
   Or reach a hand through time to catch
The far-off interest of tears?

Let Love clasp Grief lest both be drowned,
   Let darkness keep her raven gloss.
   Ah, sweeter to be drunk with loss,
To dance with Death, to beat the ground,

Than that the victor Hours should scorn
   The long result of love, and boast,

"Behold the man that loved and lost,
But all he was is overworn."

LIV

O, yet we trust that somehow good
  Will be the final goal of ill,
  To pangs of nature, sins of will,
Defects of doubt, and taints of blood;

That nothing walks with aimless feet;
  That not one life shall be destroyed,
  Or cast as rubbish to the void,
When God hath made the pile complete;

That not a worm is cloven in vain;
  That not a moth with vain desire
  Is shrivelled in a fruitless fire,
Or but subserves another's gain.

Behold, we know not anything;
  I can but trust that good shall fall
  At last—far off—at last, to all,
And every winter change to spring.

So runs my dream; but what am I?
  An infant crying in the night;
  An infant crying for the light,
And with no language but a cry.

LVI

"So careful of the type?" but no.
  From scarpèd cliff and quarried stone
  She cries, "A thousand types are gone;
I care for nothing, all shall go.

"Thou makest thine appeal to me:
  I bring to life, I bring to death;
  The spirit does but mean the breath:
I know no more." And he, shall he,

Man, her last work, who seemed so fair,
    Such splendid purpose in his eyes,
    Who rolled the psalm to wintry skies,
Who built him fanes of fruitless prayer,

Who trusted God was love indeed
    And love Creation's final law—
    Though Nature, red in tooth and claw
With ravine, shrieked against his creed—

Who loved, who suffered countless ills,
    Who battled for the True, the Just,
    Be blown about the desert dust,
Or sealed within the iron hills?

No more? A monster then, a dream,
    A discord. Dragons of the prime,
    That tare each other in their slime,
Were mellow music matched with him.

O life as futile, then, as frail!
    O for thy voice to soothe and bless!
    What hope of answer, or redress?
Behind the veil, behind the veil.

CVI

Ring out, wild bells, to the wild sky,
    The flying cloud, the frosty light:
    The year is dying in the night;
Ring out, wild bells, and let him die.

Ring out the old, ring in the new,
    Ring, happy bells across the snow:
    The year is going, let him go;
Ring out the false, ring in the true.

Ring out the grief that saps the mind,
    For those that here we see no more;
    Ring out the feud of rich and poor,
Ring in redress to all mankind.

203

Ring out a slowly dying cause,
    And ancient forms of party strife;
    Ring in the nobler modes of life,
With sweeter manners, purer laws.

Ring out the want, the care, the sin,
    The faithless coldness of the times;
    Ring out, ring out my mournful rhymes,
But ring the fuller minstrel in.

Ring out false pride in place and blood,
    The civic slander and the spite;
    Ring in the love of truth and right,
Ring in the common love of good.

Ring out old shapes of foul disease;
    Ring out the narrowing lust of gold;
    Ring out the thousand wars of old,
Ring in the thousand years of peace.

Ring in the valiant man and free,
    The larger heart, the kindlier hand;
    Ring out the darkness of the land,
Ring in the Christ that is to be.

CXXVI

Love is and was my lord and king,
    And in his presence I attend
    To hear the tidings of my friend,
Which every hour his couriers bring.

Love is and was my king and lord,
    And will be, though as yet I keep
    Within his court on earth, and sleep
Encompassed by his faithful guard,

And hear at times a sentinel
    Who moves about from place to place,
    And whispers to the worlds of space,
In the deep night, that all is well.

CXXX

Thy voice is on the rolling air;
   I hear thee where the waters run;
   Thou standest in the rising sun,
And in the setting thou art fair.

What art thou then? I cannot guess;
   But though I seem in star and flower
   To feel thee some diffusive power,
I do not therefore love thee less.

My love involves the love before;
   My love is vaster passion now;
   Though mixed with God and Nature thou,
I seem to love thee more and more.

Far off thou art, but ever nigh;
   I have thee still, and I rejoice;
   I prosper, circled with thy voice;
I shall not lose thee though I die.

CXXXI

O living will that shalt endure
   When all that seems shall suffer shock,
   Rise in the spiritual rock,
Flow through our deeds and make them pure,

That we may lift from out of dust
   A voice as unto him that hears,
   A cry above the conquered years
To one that with us works, and trust,

With faith that comes of self-control,
   The truths that never can be proved
   Until we close with all we loved,
And all we flow from, soul in soul.

Robert Browning

(1812–1889)

ABT VOGLER

*(After he has been extemporizing upon the musical instrument
of his invention)*

I

Would that the structure brave, the manifold music I build,
  Bidding my organ obey, calling its keys to their work,
Claiming each slave of the sound, at a touch, as when Solomon willed
  Armies of angels that soar, legions of demons that lurk,
Man, brute, reptile, fly,—alien of end and of aim,
  Adverse, each from the other heaven-high, hell-deep removed,—
Should rush into sight at once as he named the ineffable Name,
  And pile him a palace straight, to pleasure the princess he loved!

II

Would it might tarry like his, the beautiful building of mine,
  This which my keys in a crowd pressed and importuned to raise!
Ah, one and all, how they helped, would dispart now and now combine,
  Zealous to hasten the work, heighten their master his praise!
And one would bury his brow with a blind plunge down to hell,
  Burrow awhile and build, broad on the roots of things,
Then up again swim into sight, having based me my palace well,
  Founded it, fearless of flame, flat on the nether springs.

III

And another would mount and march, like the excellent minion he was,
  Ay, another and yet another, one crowd but with many a crest,
Raising my rampired walls of gold as transparent as glass,
  Eager to do and die, yield each his place to the rest:
For higher still and higher (as a runner tips with fire,

When a great illumination surprises a festal night—
Outlining round and round Rome's dome from space to spire)
    Up, the pinnacled glory reached, and the pride of my soul was in sight.

IV

In sight? Not half! for it seemed, it was certain, to match man's birth,
    Nature in turn conceived, obeying an impulse as I;
And the emulous heaven yearned down, made effort to reach the earth,
    As the earth had done her best, in my passion, to scale the sky:
Novel splendors burst forth, grew familiar and dwelt with mine,
    Not a point nor peak but found and fixed its wandering star;
Meteor-moons, balls of blaze: and they did not pale nor pine,
    For earth had attained to heaven, there was no more near nor far.

V

Nay more; for there wanted not who walked in the glare and glow,
    Presences plain in the place; or, fresh from the Protoplast,
Furnished for ages to come, when a kindlier wind should blow,
    Lured now to begin and live, in a house to their liking at last;
Or else the wonderful Dead who have passed through the body and
    gone,
    But were back once more to breathe in an old world worth their new:
What never had been, was now; what was, as it shall be anon;
    And what is,—shall I say, matched both? for I was made perfect too.

VI

All through my keys that gave their sounds to a wish of my soul,
    All through my soul that praised as its wish flowed visibly forth,
All through music and me! For think, had I painted the whole,
    Why, there it had stood, to see, nor the process so wonder-worth:
Had I written the same, made verse—still, effect proceeds from cause,
    Ye know why the forms are fair, ye hear how the tale is told;
It is all triumphant art, but art in obedience to laws,
    Painter and poet are proud in the artist-list enrolled:—

VII

But here is the finger of God, a flash of the will that can,
    Existent behind all laws, that made them and, lo, they are!
And I know not if, save in this, such gift be allowed to man,
    That out of three sounds he frame, not a fourth sound, but a star.
Consider it well: each tone of our scale in itself is naught;

207

It is everywhere in the world—loud, soft, and all is said:
　Give it to me to use! I mix it with two in my thought:
　　And, there! Ye have heard and seen: consider and bow the head!

VIII

Well, it is gone at last, the palace of music I reared;
　Gone! and the good tears start, the praises that come too slow;
For one is assured at first, one scarce can say that he feared,
　That he even gave it a thought, the gone thing was to go.
Never to be again! But many more of the kind
　As good, nay, better perchance: is this your comfort to me?
To me, who must be saved because I cling with my mind
　To the same, same self, same love, same God: ay, what was, shall be.

IX

Therefore to whom turn I but to thee, the ineffable Name?
　Builder and maker, thou, of houses not made with hands!
What, have fear of change from thee who art ever the same?
　Doubt that thy power can fill the heart that thy power expands?
There shall never be one lost good! What was, shall live as before;
　The evil is null, is naught, is silence implying sound;
What was good shall be good, with, for evil, so much good more;
　On the earth the broken arcs; in the heaven, a perfect round.

X

All we have willed or hoped or dreamed of good shall exist;
　Not its semblance, but itself; no beauty, nor good, nor power
Whose voice has gone forth, but each survives for the melodist
　When eternity affirms the conception of an hour.
The high that proved too high, the heroic for earth too hard,
　The passion that left the ground to lose itself in the sky,
Are music sent up to God by the lover and the bard;
　Enough that he heard it once: we shall hear it by-and-by.

XI

And what is our failure here but a triumph's evidence
　For the fulness of the days? Have we withered or agonized?
Why else was the pause prolonged but that singing might issue thence?
　Why rushed the discords in but that harmony should be prized?
Sorrow is hard to bear, and doubt is slow to clear,
　Each sufferer says his say, his scheme of the weal and woe:

But God has a few of us whom he whispers in the ear;
The rest may reason and welcome: 'tis we musicians know..

XII

Well, it is earth with me; silence resumes her reign:
I will be patient and proud, and soberly acquiesce.
Give me the keys. I feel for the common chord again,
Sliding by semitones, till I sink to the minor,—yes,
And I blunt it into a ninth, and I stand on alien ground,
Surveying awhile the heights I rolled from into the deep;
Which, hark, I have dared and done, for my resting-place is found,
The C Major of this life: so, now I will try to sleep.

Sidney Lanier

(1842–1881)

A BALLAD OF TREES AND THE MASTER

Into the woods my Master went,
Clean forspent, forspent.
Into the woods my Master came,
Forspent with love and shame.
But the olives they were not blind to Him,
The little gray leaves were kind to Him;
The thorn-tree had a mind to Him
When into the woods He came.

Out of the woods my Master went,
And he was well content.
Out of the woods my Master came,
Content with death and shame.
When Death and Shame would woo Him last
From under the trees they drew Him last;
'Twas on a tree they slew Him—last
When out of the woods He came.

Anonymous

(American Negro Spirituals)

WERE YOU THERE . . . ?

Were you there when they crucified my Lord?
Were you there when they crucified my Lord?
Oh! Sometimes it causes me to tremble, tremble, tremble.
Were you there when they crucified my Lord?

Were you there when they nailed him to the tree?
Were you there when they nailed him to the tree?
Oh! Sometimes it causes me to tremble, tremble, tremble.
Were you there when they nailed him to the tree?

Were you there, when they pierced him in the side?
Were you there, when they pierced him in the side?
Oh, sometimes, it causes me to tremble, tremble, tremble.
Were you there, when they pierced him in the side?

Were you there, when the sun refused to shine?
Were you there, when the sun refused to shine?
Oh, sometimes, it causes me to tremble, tremble, tremble.
Were you there, when the sun refused to shine?

Were you there when they laid him in the tomb?
Were you there when they laid him in the tomb?
Oh! Sometimes it causes me to tremble, tremble, tremble.
Were you there when they laid him in the tomb?

GIVE ME JESUS

Oh, when I come to die,
Oh, when I come to die,
Oh, when I come to die,
Give me Jesus.

210

In that mornin' when I rise,
That mornin' when I rise,
In that mornin' when I rise,
Give me Jesus.

Give me Jesus, give me Jesus,
You may have all this world, give me Jesus,
Oh, give me Jesus, give me Jesus,
You may have all this world, give me Jesus.

Dark midnight was my cry,
Dark midnight was my cry,
Dark midnight was my cry,
Give me Jesus.
I heard a mourner say,
I heard a mourner say,
I heard a mourner say,
Give me Jesus.

DEEP RIVER

Deep river, my home is over Jordan,
Deep river, Lord; I want to cross over into camp ground.

O children, O, don't you want to go to that gospel feast,
That promised land, that land, where all is peace?

Deep river, my home is over Jordan,
Deep river, Lord; I want to cross over into camp ground.

Oscar Wilde

(1856–1900)

E TENEBRIS

Come down, O Christ, and help me! reach thy hand,
   For I am drowning in a stormier sea
   Than Simon on thy lake of Galilee:
The wine of life is spilt upon the sand,
My heart is as some famine-murdered land
   Whence all good things have perished utterly,
   And well I know my soul in Hell must lie
If I this night before God's throne should stand.
"He sleeps perchance, or rideth to the chase,
   Like Baal, when his prophets howled that name
   From morn to noon on Carmel's smitten height."
Nay, peace, I shall behold, before the night,
   The feet of brass, the robe more white than flame,
The wounded hands, the weary human face.

Francis Thompson

(1859–1907)

"IN NO STRANGE LAND"

O world invisible, we view thee,
O world intangible, we touch thee,
O world unknowable, we know thee,
Inapprehensible, we clutch thee!

Does the fish soar to find the ocean,
The eagle plunge to find the air—
That we ask of the stars in motion
If they have rumor of thee there?

212

Not where the wheeling systems darken,
And our benumbered conceiving soars!—
The drift of pinions, would we hearken,
Beats at our own clay-shuttered doors.

The angels keep their ancient places;—
Turn but a stone, and start a wing!
'Tis ye, 'tis your estrangéd faces,
That miss the many-splendored thing.

But (when so sad thou canst not sadder)
Cry—and upon thy so sore loss
Shall shine the traffic of Jacob's ladder
Pitched betwixt Heaven and Charing Cross.

Yea, in the night, my Soul, my daughter,
Cry—clinging Heaven by the hems;
And lo, Christ walking on the water
Not of Gennesareth, but Thames!

part eight

Modern Christian Poems

"Let him easter in us, be a dayspring to the dimness of us. . . ."

The phoenix, a mythical bird, is a symbol of the Resurrection. It is mentioned in *First Clement*, an early post-apostolic letter, as a bird that is reborn from its own ashes every five hundred years.

Gerard Manley Hopkins

(1844–1889)

THE WRECK OF THE DEUTSCHLAND

To the happy memory of five Franciscan Nuns
exiles by the Falk Laws
drowned between midnight and morning of Dec. 7th 1875

PART THE FIRST

1

    Thou mastering me
   God! giver of breath and bread;
  World's strand, sway of the sea;
   Lord of living and dead;
Thou hast bound bones and veins in me, fastened me flesh,
And after it almost unmade, what with dread,
  Thy doing: and dost thou touch me afresh?
Over again I feel thy finger and find thee.

2

    I did say yes
   O at lightning and lashed rod;
  Thou heardst me truer than tongue confess
   Thy terror, O Christ, O God;
Thou knowest the walls, altar and hour and night:
The swoon of a heart that the sweep and the hurl of thee trod
  Hard down with a horror of height:
And the midriff astrain with leaning of, laced with fire of stress.

217

The frown of his face
Before me, the hurtle of hell
Behind, where, where was a, where was a place?
I whirled out wings that spell
And fled with a fling of the heart to the heart of the Host.
My heart, but you were dovewinged, I can tell,
Carrier-witted, I am bold to boast,
To flash from the flame to the flame then, tower from the grace to the
grace.

4

I am soft sift
In an hourglass—at the wall
Fast, but mined with a motion, a drift,
And it crowds and it combs to the fall;
I steady as a water in a well, to a poise, to a pane,
But roped with, always, all the way down from the tall
Fells or flanks of the voel, a vein
Of the gospel proffer, a pressure, a principle, Christ's gift.

I kiss my hand
To the stars, lovely-asunder
Starlight, wafting him out of it; and
Glow, glory in thunder;
Kiss my hand to the dappled-with-damson west:
Since, tho' he is under the world's splendour and wonder,
His mystery must be instressed, stressed;
For I greet him the days I meet him, and bless when I understand.

6

Not out of his bliss
Springs the stress felt
Nor first from heaven (and few know this)
Swings the stroke dealt—
Stroke and a stress that stars and storms deliver,

That guilt is hushed by, hearts are flushed by and melt—
　　But it rides time like riding a river
(And here the faithful waver, the faithless fable and miss).

7

　　It dates from day
　　　Of his going in Galilee;
　　Warm-laid grave of a womb-life grey;
　　　Manger, maiden's knee;
The dense and the driven Passion, and frightful sweat;
Thence the discharge of it, there its swelling to be,
　　Though felt before, though in high flood yet—
What none would have known of it, only the heart, being hard at bay,

8

　　Is out with it! Oh,
　　　We lash with the best or worst
　　Word last! How a lush-kept plush-capped sloe
　　　Will, mouthed to flesh-burst,
Gush!—flush the man, the being with it, sour or sweet,
Brim, in a flash, full!—Hither then, last or first,
　　To hero of Calvary, Christ's feet—
Never ask if meaning it, wanting it, warned of it—men go.

9

　　Be adored among men,
　　　God, three-numberèd form;
　　Wring thy rebel, dogged in den,
　　　Man's malice, with wrecking and storm.
Beyond saying sweet, past telling of tongue,
Thou art lightning and love, I found it, a winter and warm;
　　Father and fondler of heart thou hast wrung:
Hast thy dark descending and most art merciful then.

With an anvil-ding
And with fire in him forge thy will
Or rather, rather then, stealing as Spring
    Through him, melt him but master him still:
Whether at once, as once at a crash Paul,
Or as Austin, a lingering-out swéet skill,
    Make mercy in all of us, out of us all
Mastery, but be adored, but be adored King.

PART THE SECOND

11

'Some find me a sword; some
The flange and the rail; flame,
Fang, or flood' goes Death on drum,
    And storms bugle his fame.
But wé dream we are rooted in earth—Dust!
Flesh falls within sight of us, we, though our flower the same,
    Wave with the meadow, forget that there must
The sour scythe cringe, and the blear share come.

12

On Saturday sailed from Bremen,
American-outward-bound,
Take settler and seamen, tell men with women,
    Two hundred souls in the round—
O Father, not under thy feathers nor ever as guessing
The goal was a shoal, of a fourth the doom to be drowned;
    Yet did the dark side of the bay of thy blessing
Not vault them, the million of rounds of thy mercy not reeve even
    them in?

13

Into the snows she sweeps,
Hurling the haven behind,
The Deutschland, on Sunday; and so the sky keeps,

For the infinite air is unkind,
And the sea flint-flake, black-backed in the regular blow,
Sitting Eastnortheast, in cursed quarter, the wind;
Wiry and white-fiery and whirlwind-swivellèd snow
Spins to the widow-making unchilding unfathering deeps.

14

She drove in the dark to leeward,
She struck—not a reef or a rock
But the combs of a smother of sand: night drew her
Dead to the Kentish Knock;
And she beat the bank down with her bows and the ride of her
keel:
The breakers rolled on her beam with ruinous shock;
And canvas and compass, the whorl and the wheel
Idle for ever to waft her or wind her with, these she endured.

15

Hope had grown grey hairs,
Hope had mourning on,
Trenched with tears, carved with cares,
Hope was twelve hours gone;
And frightful a nightfall folded rueful a day
Nor rescue, only rocket and lightship, shone,
And lives at last were washing away:
To the shrouds they took,—they shook in the hurling and horrible airs.

16

One stirred from the rigging to save
The wild woman-kind below,
With a rope's end round the man, handy and brave—
He was pitched to his death at a blow,
For all his dreadnought breast and braids of thew:
They could tell him for hours, dandled the to and fro
Through the cobbled foam-fleece, what could he do
With the burl of the fountains of air, buck and the flood of the wave?

17

They fought with God's cold—
And they could not and fell to the deck
(Crushed them) or water (and drowned them) or rolled
With the sea-romp over the wreck.
Night roared, with the heart-break hearing a heart-broke rabble,
The woman's wailing, the crying of child without check—
Till a lioness arose breasting the babble,
A prophetess towered in the tumult, a virginal tongue told.

Ah, touched in your bower of bone
Are you! turned for an exquisite smart,
Have you! make words break from me here all alone,
Do you!—mother of being in me, heart.
O unteachably after evil, but uttering truth,
Why, tears! is it? tears; such a melting, a madrigal start!
Never-eldering revel and river of youth,
What can it be, this glee? the good you have there of your own?

19

Sister, a sister calling
A master, her master and mine!—
And the inboard seas run swirling and hawling;
The rash smart sloggering brine
Blinds her; but she that weather sees one thing, one;
Has one fetch in her: she rears herself to divine
Ears, and the call of the tall nun
To the men in the tops and the tackle rode over the storm's brawling.

She was first of a five and came
Of a coifèd sisterhood.
(O Deutschland, double a desperate name!
O world wide of its good!
But Gertrude, lily, and Luther, are two of a town,

Christ's lily and beast of the waste wood:
  From life's dawn it is drawn down,
Abel is Cain's brother and breasts they have sucked the same.)

21

  Loathed for a love men knew in them,
    Banned by the land of their birth,
  Rhine refused them. Thames would ruin them;
    Surf, snow, river and earth
Gnashed: but thou art above, thou Orion of light;
Thy unchancelling poising palms were weighing the worth,
  Thou martyr-master: in thy sight
Storm flakes were scroll-leaved flowers, lily showers—sweet heaven was
  astrew in them.

22

  Five! the finding and sake
  And cipher of suffering Christ.
  Mark, the mark is of man's make
  And the word of it Sacrificed.
But he scores it in scarlet himself on his own bespoken,
Before-time-taken, dearest prizèd and priced—
  Stigma, signal, cinquefoil token
For lettering of the lamb's fleece, ruddying of the rose flake.

23

  Joy fall to thee, father Francis,
    Drawn to the Life that died;
  With the gnarls of the nails in thee, niche of the lance, his
    Lovescape crucified
And seal of his seraph-arrival! and these thy daughters
and five-livèd and leavèd favour and pride,
  Are sisterly sealed in wild waters,
To bathe in his fall-gold mercies, to breathe in his all-fire glances.

24

Away in the lovable west,
  On a pastoral forehead of Wales,
I was under a roof here, I was at rest,
  And they the prey of the gales;
She to the black-about air, to the breaker, the thickly
Falling flakes, to the throng that catches and quails
  Was calling 'O Christ, Christ, come quickly':
The cross to her she calls Christ to her, christens her wild-worst Best.

25

The majesty! what did she mean?
  Breathe, arch and original Breath.
Is it love in her of the being as her lover had been?
  Breathe, body of lovely Death.
They were else-minded then, altogether, the men
Woke thee with a *we are perishing* in the weather of Gennesareth.
  Or is it that she cried for the crown then,
The keener to come at the comfort for feeling the combating keen?

26

For how to the heart's cheering
  The down-dugged ground-hugged grey
Hovers off, the jay-blue heavens appearing
  Of pied and peeled May!
Blue-beating and hoary-glow height; or night, still higher,
With belled fire and the moth-soft Milky Way,
  What by your measure is the heaven of desire,
The treasure never eyesight got, nor was ever guessed what for the
  hearing?

27

No, but it was not these.
  The jading and jar of the cart,
Time's tasking, it is fathers that asking for ease
  Of the sodden-with-its-sorrowing heart,

Not danger, electrical horror; then further it finds
The appealing of the Passion is tenderer in prayer apart:
   Other, I gather, in measure her mind's
Burden, in wind's burly and beat of endragonèd seas.

28

   But how shall I . . . make me room there:
   Reach me a . . . Fancy, come faster—
  Strike you the sight of it? look at it loom there,
   Thing that she . . . there then! the Master,
Ipse the only one, Christ, King, Head:
He was to cure the extremity where he had cast her;
   Do, deal, lord it with living and dead;
Let him ride, her pride, in his triumph, despatch and have done with
   his doom there.

29

   Ah! there was a heart right!
   There was single eye!
  Read the unshapeable shock night
   And knew the who and the why;
Wording it how but by him that present and past,
Heaven and earth are word of, worded by?—
   The Simon Peter of a soul! to the blast
Tarpeïan-fast, but a blown beacon of light.

30

   Jesu, heart's light,
   Jesu, maid's son,
  What was the feast followed the night
   Thou hadst glory of this nun?—
Feast of the one woman without stain.
For so conceivèd, so to conceive thee is done;
   But here was heart-throe, birth of a brain,
Word, that heard and kept thee and uttered thee outright.

31

Well, she has thee for the pain, for the
Patience; but pity of the rest of them!
Heart, go and bleed at a bitterer vein for the
Comfortless unconfessed of them—
No not uncomforted: lovely-felicitous Providence
Finger of a tender of, O of a feathery delicacy, the breast of the
Maiden could obey so, be a bell to, ring of it, and
Startle the poor sheep back! is the shipwrack then a harvest, does
tempest carry the grain for thee?

32

I admire thee, master of the tides,
Of the Yore-flood, of the year's fall;
The recurb and the recovery of the gulf's sides,
The girth of it and the wharf of it and the wall;
Stanching, quenching ocean of a motionable mind;
Ground of being, and granite of it: past all
Grasp God, throned behind
Death with a sovereignty that heeds but hides, bodes but abides;

With a mercy that outrides
The all of water, an ark
For the listener; for the lingerer with a love glides
Lower than death and the dark;
A vein for the visiting of the past-prayer, pent in prison,
The-last-breath penitent spirits—the uttermost mark
Our passion–plungèd giant risen,
The Christ of the Father compassionate, fetched in the storm of his
strides.

34

Now burn, new born to the world,
Double-naturèd name,
The heaven-flung, heart-fleshed, maiden-furled
Miracle-in-Mary-of-flame,

Mid-numberèd He in three of the thunder-throne!
Not a dooms-day dazzle in his coming nor dark as he came;
   Kind, but royally reclaiming his own;
A released shower, let flash to the shire, not a lightning of fire hard-
    hurled.

35

   Dame, at our door
Drowned, and among our shoals,
  Remember us in the roads, the heaven-haven of the Reward:
   Our King back, oh, upon English souls!
Let him easter in us, be a dayspring to the dimness of us, be a
    crimson-cresseted east,
More brightening her, rare-dear Britain, as his reign rolls,
   Pride, rose, prince, hero of us, high-priest,
Our hearts' charity's hearth's fire, our thoughts' chivalry's throng's
    Lord.

Paul Verlaine

(1844–1896)

A CONFESSION

O my God, Thou has wounded me with love,
Behold the wound that is still vibrating.
O my God, Thou has wounded me with love.

O my God, Thy fear hath fallen upon me,
Behold the burn is there and it throbs aloud.
O my God, Thy fear hath fallen upon me.

O my God, I have known all that is vile,
And Thy glory hath stationed itself in me.
O my God, I have known all that is vile.

Drown my soul in floods, floods of Thy wine,
Mingle my life with the body of Thy bread.
Drown my soul in floods, floods of Thy wine.

227

Take my blood that I have not poured out,
Take my flesh unworthy of Thy suffering,
Take my blood that I have not poured out.

Take my brow that has only learned to blush,
To be the footstool of Thine adorable feet,
Take my brow that has only learned to blush.

Take my hands because they have labored not,
For coals of fire and for rare frankincense,
Take my hands because they have labored not.

Take my heart that has beaten for vain things,
To throb under the thorns of Calvary,
Take my heart that has beaten for vain things.

Take my feet, frivolous travellers,
That they may run to the crying of Thy grace,
Take my feet, frivolous travellers.

Take my voice, a harsh and lying noise,
For the reproaches of Thy penitence,
Take my voice, a harsh and lying noise.

Take mine eyes, luminaries of deceit,
That they may be extinguished in tears of prayer,
Take mine eyes, luminaries of deceit.

Ah, Thou God of pardon and promises,
What is the pit of mine ingratitude!
Ah, Thou God of pardon and promises.

God of terror and God of holiness,
Alas, my sinfulness is a black abyss!
God of terror, God of holiness.

Thou God of peace, of joy and delight,
All my tears, all my ignorances,
Thou God of peace, of joy and delight.

Thou, O God, knowest all this, all this,
How poor I am, poorer than any man,

Thou, O God, knowest this, all this.
And what I have, my God, I give to Thee.

From the French, by Arthur Symons

Miguel de Unamuno

(1864–1936)

THE CHRIST OF VELÁZQUEZ: From Part One

> *My beloved is white . . .*
> Song of Songs 5:10

Of what art Thou thinking, oh my dead Christ?
And why does that heavy curtain of night,
the abundant black hair of a Nazarite
fall over thy forehead? Thou look'st within,
there where is the kingdom of God, within
Thyself, there where dawns the eternal sun
of living souls. Thy body is as white
as the mirror of the father of light,
the sun, life-giver; thy body is white
as is the moon, that dead revolves around
its mother, our tired wandering earth;
thy body is white as the host of heaven
of sovereign night, of that heaven as black
as the veil of thine abundant black hair
of a Nazarite.
    For Thou art the Christ,
the only Man who did willingly die,
the conqueror over death, that to life
through Thee was elevated. And since then
through Thee that death of thine gives to us life,
through Thee death has been made for us a mother,
through Thee death is the welcome, kindly aid
that sweetens the bitterness of our life,
through Thee, the Man dead, He that does not die,

white like the moon of night. Life is a sleep,
Christ, and death is a vigil. While the earth
is sleeping alone, the white moon keeps watch;
from his cross the Man keeps watch while men sleep;
the bloodless Man keeps vigil, the Man white
as is the moon of the black night; He watches,
the Man who gave all of his blood that men
might know that they are men. Thou didst save death,
thine arms open to the night which is black
and most beautiful, for the sun of life
has looked upon it with his eyes of fire:
for the dark night was made so by the sun,
made so beautiful. And the lonely moon,
the white moon, is beautiful in the star-lit
night that is black as the abundant black
hair of the Nazarite. The moon is white
as the body of the Man on the cross,
that is the mirror of the sun of life,
the sun of life that never, never dies.

Oh Master, the rays of thy quiet light
guide us in the dark night of this our world,
strengthening us with the enduring hope
of an eternal day! Fond night, oh night,
mother of tender dreams, mother of hope,
oh most gentle night, dark night of the soul,
thou art nurse of our hope in Christ the Saviour!

From the Spanish, by Eleanor L. Turnbull

Edwin Arlington Robinson

(1869–1935)

CALVARY

Friendless and faint, with martyred steps and slow,
Faint for the flesh, but for the spirit free,
Stung by the mob that came to see the show,
The Master toiled along to Calvary;
We gibed him, as he went, with houndish glee,
Till his dimmed eyes for us did overflow;
We cursed his vengeless hands thrice wretchedly,—
And this was nineteen hundred years ago.

But after nineteen hundred years the shame
Still clings, and we have not made good the loss
That outraged faith has entered in his name.
Ah, when shall come love's courage to be strong!
Tell me, O Lord—tell me, O Lord, how long
Are we to keep Christ writhing on the cross!

William Butler Yeats

(1865–1939)

THE SECOND COMING

Turning and turning in the widening gyre
The falcon cannot hear the falconer;
Things fall apart; the centre cannot hold;
Mere anarchy is loosed upon the world,
The blood-dimmed tide is loosed, and everywhere
The ceremony of innocence is drowned;

The best lack all conviction, while the worst
Are full of passionate intensity.

Surely some revelation is at hand;
Surely the Second Coming is at hand.
The Second Coming! Hardly are those words out
When a vast image out of *Spiritus Mundi*
Troubles my sight: somewhere in sands of the desert
A shape with lion body and the head of a man,
A gaze blank and pitiless as the sun,
Is moving its slow thighs, while all about it
Reel shadows of the indignant desert birds.
The darkness drops again; but now I know
That twenty centuries of stony sleep
Were vexed to nightmare by a rocking cradle,
And what rough beast, its hour come round at last,
Slouches towards Bethlehem to be born?

Charles Péguy

(1873–1914)

From NIGHT

God speaks:

Nights follow each other and are linked, and for the child nights are
    continuous and are the innermost part of his very being.
Therein does he fall back. They are the innermost part of his life,
They are his very being. Night is the place, night is the being wherein
    he bathes, and is nourished, and is created, and is made,
Wherein he accomplishes his being,
Wherein he recovers his strength.
Night is the place, night is the being wherein he rests, wherein he
    retires, wherein he collects himself,
Wherein he enters again. And he comes out refreshed. Night is my
    most beautiful creation.

Now why doesn't man make use of it. I am told that there are men who
  don't sleep at night.
Night, for my children and for my young
Hope, is what it really is. It is the children who see and who know.
  It is my young hope
Who sees and who knows. Who knows what being means,
What the being called night is. Night it is that continues.
Children know very well. Children see very well.
And it is the days that are discontinuous. It is the days that pierce, that
  disrupt night,
And in no wise the nights that interrupt day.
It is day that troubles night with its noise,
Otherwise night would sleep.
And the solitude, and the silence of night is so beautiful and so great
That it surrounds and corners and buries the days themselves,
That it makes an august enclosure around the restlessness of days.
Children are right, my little hope is right. All nights together
Meet and join as in a beautiful roundelay, as in a beautiful dance,
A dance of nights holding each other by the hand, whereas lead days
Make nothing more than a procession in which hands are not joined.

From the French, by Ann and Julian Green

Rainer Maria Rilke

(1875–1926)

BIRTH OF MARY

O what must it have cost the angels
not suddenly to burst into song, as one bursts into tears,
since indeed they knew: on this night the mother is being
born to the boy, the One, who shall soon appear.

Soaring they held themselves silent and showed the direction
where, alone, Joachim's farm lay;

ah, they felt in themselves and in space the pure precipitation,
but none might go down to him.

For the two were already quite beside themselves with ado.
A neighbor-woman came and played wise and did not know how,
and the old man, carefully, went and withheld the mooing
Of a dark cow. For so it had never yet been.

From the German, by M. D. Herter Norton

JOSEPH'S SUSPICION

And the angel spoke and made an effort
with the man, who clenched his fists;
But dost thou not see by every fold
that she is cool as God's early day?

Yet the other looked somberly at him,
murmuring only: What has changed her so?
But at that the angel cried: Carpenter,
dost thou not yet see that the Lord God is acting?

Because thou makest boards, in thy pride,
wouldst thou really call him to account
who modestly out of the same wood
makes leaves burgeon and buds swell?

He understood. And as he now raised his eyes
very frightened, to the angel,
he was gone. He pushed his heavy
cap slowly off. Then he sang praise.

From the German, by M. D. Herter Norton

T. S. Eliot

(1888–1965)

JOURNEY OF THE MAGI

'A cold coming we had of it,
Just the worst time of the year
For a journey, and such a long journey:
The ways deep and the weather sharp,
The very dead of winter.'
And the camels galled, sore-footed, refractory,
Lying down in the melting snow.
There were times we regretted
The summer palaces on slopes, the terraces,
And the silken girls bringing sherbet.
Then the camel men cursing and grumbling
And running away, and wanting their liquor and women,
And the night-fires going out, and the lack of shelters,
And the cities hostile and the towns unfriendly
And the villages dirty and charging high prices:
A hard time we had of it.
At the end we preferred to travel all night,
Sleeping in snatches,
With the voices singing in our ears, saying
That this was all folly.

Then at dawn we came down to a temperate valley,
Wet, below the snow line, smelling of vegetation;
With a running stream and a water-mill beating the darkness,
And three trees on the low sky,
And an old white horse galloped away in the meadow.
Then we came to a tavern with vine-leaves over the lintel,
Six hands at an open door dicing for pieces of silver,
And feet kicking the empty wine-skins.

But there was no information, and so we continued
And arrived at evening, not a moment too soon
Finding the place; it was (you may say) satisfactory.

All this was a long time ago, I remember,
And I would do it again, but set down
This set down
This: were we led all that way for
Birth or Death? There was a Birth, certainly,
We had evidence and no doubt. I had seen birth and death,
But had thought they were different; this Birth was
Hard and bitter agony for us, like Death, our death.
We returned to our places, these Kingdoms,
But no longer at ease here, in the old dispensation,
With an alien people clutching their gods.
I should be glad of another death.

Boris Pasternak

(1890–1960)

EVIL DAYS

When He was entering Jerusalem
During that last week
He was hailed with thunderous hosannas;
The people ran in His wake, waving palm branches.

Yet the days were becoming ever more ominous, more grim.
There was no stirring the hearts of men through love:
Their eyebrows knit in disdain.
And now, the epilogue. Finis.

The heavens lay heavy over the houses,
Crushing with all of their leaden weight.
The Pharisees were seeking evidence against Him,
Yet cringed before Him like foxes.

Then the dark forces of the Temple
Gave Him up to be judged by the offscourings.
And, with the same fervor with which they once sang His praises,
Men now reviled Him.

The rabble from the vicinity
Was peering in at the gateway.
They kept jostling as they bided the outcome,
Surging, receding.

The neighborhood crawled with sly whispers
And rumors crept in from all sides.
He recalled the flight into Egypt and His childhood
But recalled them now as in a dream.

He remembered the majestic cliffside in the wilderness
And that exceeding high mountain
Whereon Satan had tempted Him,
Offering Him all the kingdoms of the world.

And the marriage feast at Cana
And the guests in great admiration over the miracle.
And the sea on which, in a mist,
He had walked to the boat as if over dry land.

And the gathering of the poor in a hovel
And His going down into a cellar by the light of a taper
Which had suddenly gone out in affright
When the man risen from the dead was trying to get to his feet.

From the Russian, by Bernard Guilbert Guerney

e. e. cummings

(1894–1962)

WHEN GOD LETS MY BODY BE

when god lets my body be

From each brave eye shall sprout a tree
fruit that dangles therefrom

the purpled world will dance upon
Between my lips which did sing

a rose shall beget the spring
that maidens whom passion wastes

will lay between their little breasts
My strong fingers beneath the snow

into strenuous birds shall go
my love walking in the grass

their wings will touch with her face
and all the while shall my heart be

With the bulge and nuzzle of the sea

W. H. Auden

(1907–   )

WHITSUNDAY IN KIRCHSTETTEN
(for H. A. Reinhold)

Grace dances. I would pipe. Dance ye all.
                                    Acts of John

Komm Schöpfer Geist I bellow as Herr Beer
picks up our slim offerings and Pfarrer Lustkandl
    quietly gets on with the Sacrifice
as Rome does it: outside car-worshipers enact
    the ritual exodus from Vienna
their successful cult demands (though reckoning time
    by the Jewish week and the Christian year
like their pedestrian fathers). When Mass is over,
    although obedient to Canterbury,
I shall be well gruss-gotted, asked to contribute
    to *Caritas,* though a metic come home
to lunch on my own land: no doubt, if the Allies had not
    conquered the Ost-Mark, if the dollar fell,
the *Gemütlichkeit* would be less, but when was peace
    or its concomitant smile the worse
for being undeserved?

                In the onion-tower overhead
    bells clash at the Elevation, calling
on Austria to change: whether the world has improved
    is doubtful, but we believe it could
and the divine Tiberius didn't. Rejoice, the bells
    cry to me. Blake's Old Nobodaddy
in his astronomic telescopic heaven,
    the Big White Christian upstairs, is dead,

239

and won't come hazing us no more, nor bless our bombs:
    no more need sons of the menalty,
divining their future from plum stones, count aloud
    Army, Navy, Law, Church, nor a Prince
say who is *papabile.* (The Ape of the Living God
    knows how to stage a funeral, though,
as penitents like it: Babel, like Sodom, still
    has plenty to offer, though of course it draws
a better sort of crowd.) Rejoice: we who were born
    congenitally deaf are able
to listen now to rank outsiders. The Holy Ghost
    does not abhor a golfer's jargon,
a Lower-Austrian accent, the cadences even
    of my own little Anglo-American
musico-literary set (though difficult,
    saints at least may think in algebra
without sin): but no sacred nonsense can stand Him.
    Our magic syllables melt away,
our tribal formulae are laid bare: since this morning,
    it is with a vocabulary
made wholesomely profane, open in lexicons
    to our foes to translate, that we endeavor
each in his idiom to express the true *magnalia*
    which need no hallowing from us, loaning terms,
exchanging graves and legends. (Maybe, when just now
    Kirchstetten prayed for the dead, only I
remembered Franz Joseph the Unfortunate, who danced
    once in eighty-six years and never
used the telephone.)

        An altar bell makes a noise
    as the Body of the Second Adam
is shown to some of his torturers, forcing them
    to visualize absent enemies
with the same right to grow hybrid corn and be wicked
    as an Abendlander. As crows fly,
ninety kilometers from here our habits end,

where minefield and watchtower say NO EXIT
from peace-loving Crimtartary, except for crows
   and agents of peace: from Loipersbach
to the Bering Sea not a living stockbroker,
   and church attendance is frowned upon
like visiting brothels (but the chess and physics
   are still the same). We shall bury you
and dance at the wake, say her chiefs: that, says Reason
   is unlikely. But to most people
I'm the wrong color: it could be the looter's turn
   for latrine duty and the flogging block,
my kin who trousered Africa, carried our smell
   to germless poles.
          Down a Gothic nave
comes our Pfarrer now, blessing the West with water:
   we may go. There is no Queen's English
in any context for *Geist* or *Esprit:* about
   catastrophe or how to behave in one
I know nothing, except what everyone knows—
   if there when Grace dances, I should dance.

Stephen Spender

(1909–   )

JUDAS ISCARIOT

The eyes of twenty centuries
Pursue me along corridors to where
I am painted at their ends on many walls.
   Ever-revolving futures recognize
This red hair and red beard, where I am seated
Within the dark cave of the feast of light.
   Out of my heart-shaped shadow I stretch my hand
Across the white table into the dish
But not to dip the bread. It is as though
The cloth on each side of one dove-bright face

Spread dazzling wings on which the apostles ride
Uplifting them into the vision
Where their eyes watch themselves enthroned
   My russet hand across the dish
Plucks enviously against one feather
   —But still the rushing wings spurn me below!

   Saint Sebastian of wickedness
I stand: all eyes legitimate arrows piercing through
The darkness of my wickedness. They recognize
My halo hammered from thirty silver pieces
And the hemp rope around my neck
Soft as that spirit's hanging arms
When on my cheek he answered with the kiss
Which cuts for ever—
          My strange stigmata,
All love and hate, all fire and ice!

   But who betrayed whom? O you,
Whose light gaze forms the azure corridor
Through which those other pouring eyes
Arrow into me—answer! Who
Betrayed whom? Who had foreseen
All, from the first? Who read
In his mind's light from the first day
That the kingdom of heaven on earth must always
Reiterate the garden of Eden,
And each day's revolution be betrayed
Within man's heart each day?
         Who wrapped
The whispering serpent round the tree
And hung between the leaves the glittering purse
And trapped the fangs with God-appointed poison?
Who knew
I must betray the truth, and made the lie
Betray its truth in me?

   Those hypocrite eyes which aimed at you
Now aim at me. And yet, beyond this world

We are alone, eternal opposites,
Each turning on his pole of truth, your pole
Invisible light, and mine
Becoming what man is. We stare
Across two thousand years, and heaven, and hell,
Into each other's gaze.

Czeslaw Milosz

(1911–   )

A POOR CHRISTIAN LOOKS AT THE GHETTO

Bees build around red liver,
Ants build around black bone.
It has begun: the tearing, the trampling on silks,
It has begun: the breaking of glass, wood, copper, nickel, silver, foam

Of gypsum, iron sheets, violin strings, trumpets, leaves, balls, crystals.
Poof! Phosphorescent fire from yellow walls
Engulfs animal and human hair.

Bees build around the honeycomb of lungs,
Ants build around white bone.
Torn is paper, rubber, linen, leather, flax,
Fibre, fabrics, cellulose, snakeskin, wire.
The roof and the wall collapse in flame and heat seizes the foundations.
Now there is only the earth, sandy, trodden down,
With one leafless tree.

Slowly, boring a tunnel, a guardian mole makes his way,
With a small red lamp fastened to his forehead.
He touches burned bodies, counts them, pushes on,
He distinguishes human ashes by their luminous vapour,
The ashes of each man by a different part of the spectrum.
Bees build around a red trace.

Ants build around the place left by my body.

I am afraid, so afraid of the guardian mole.
He has swollen eyelids, like a Patriarch
Who has sat much in the light of candles
Reading the great book of the species.
What will I tell him, I, a Jew of the New Testament,
Waiting two thousand years for the second coming of Jesus?
My broken body will deliver me to his sight
And he will count me among the helpers of death:
The uncircumcised.

From the Polish, by Czeslaw Milosz

Dylan Thomas

(1914–1953)

AND DEATH SHALL HAVE NO DOMINION

And death shall have no dominion.
Dead men naked they shall be one
With the man in the wind and the west moon;
When their bones are picked clean and the clean bones gone,
They shall have stars at elbow and foot;
Though they go mad they shall be sane,
Though they sink through the sea they shall rise again;
Though lovers be lost love shall not;
And death shall have no dominion.

And death shall have no dominion.
Under the windings of the sea
They lying long shall not die windily;
Twisting on racks when sinews give way,
Strapped to a wheel, yet they shall not break;
Faith in their hands shall snap in two,
And the unicorn evils run them through;
Split all ends up they shan't crack;
And death shall have no dominion.

And death shall have no dominion.
No more may gulls cry at their ears
Or waves break loud on the seashores;
Where blew a flower may a flower no more
Lift its head to the blows of the rain;
Though they be mad and dead as nails,
Heads of the characters hammer through daisies;
Break in the sun till the sun breaks down,
And death shall have no dominion.

Robert Lowell

(1917–   )

THE HOLY INNOCENTS

Listen, the hay-bells tinkle as the cart
Wavers on rubber tires along the tar
And cindered ice below the burlap mill
And ale-wife run. The oxen drool and start
In wonder at the fenders of a car
And blunder hugely up St. Peter's hill.
These are the undefiled by woman—their
Sorrow is not the sorrow of this world:
King Herod shrieking vengeance at the curled
Up knees of Jesus choking in the air,

A king of speechless clods and infants. Still
The world out-Herods Herod; and the year,
The nineteen-hundred forty-fifth of grace,
Lumbers with losses up the clinkered hill
Of our purgation; and the oxen near
The worn foundations of their resting place,
The holy manger where their bed is corn
And holly torn for Christmas. If they die,
As Jesus, in the harness, who will mourn?
Lamb of the shepherds, Child, how still you lie.

Vassar Miller

(1924–   )

DEFENSE RESTS

I want
a love to hold
in my hand because love
is too much for the heart to bear
alone.

Then stop
mouthing to me
"Faith and Sacraments" when
the Host feather-heavy weighs down
my soul.

So I
blaspheme! My Lord,
John's head on your breast or
Mary's lips on your feet, would you
agree?

If this
is not enough—
upon Your sweat, Your thirst,
Your nails, and nakedness I rest
my case.

Dale Driscoll

(1939–   )

SAINT FRANCIS PREACHING TO THE BIRDS
(after Giotto's fresco)

what strange sound of voice con-
founded you
where blood and hunt are bound
to bring you sparrowhawk
acquiescent to his feet

a feathery nimbus you traced a-
bout the spot he stood
arms upraised untethered be-
fore the autumn woods

in the moment of a drifting leaf
you flew deep within his fold of arms
and the place where you had spaced your feet
gave way to an-
other nimbus
thorny rimmed

and
together saint and bird
you made the day
stand spot-
less still

Index of Poets

Index of Poems

252

Index of First Lines

254

256

72 73 10 9 8 7 6 5 4 3 2 1